101

Swimming Pool
Games & Activities

Jared R. Knight

Disclaimer
Every effort was made to ensure that this book featured safe activities and programs for participants, including a detailed list of the proper use of equipment and recommendations for the size of the group, age range, swimming level, and safety precautions for each game. The author and publisher specifically disclaim any liability arising from the use of any information in this book.

ISBN: 978-1-60679-096-0
Library of Congress Control Number: 2010921900
Cover design: Brenden Murphy
Book layout: Deb Oldenburg
Front cover photo: Jared R. Knight
Back cover photo: Charlee Allen

Healthy Learning
P.O. Box 1828
Monterey, CA 93942
www.healthylearning.com

Dedication

Dedicated to Rachel, Alex, and Emerson.

Acknowledgments

I would like to thank my family and the editors and friends at Healthy Learning and the American Camp Association for their support and encouragement. Special thanks to the camp counselors at Aspen Grove Family Camp for their enthusiasm in playing these games during the summer in preparation for this book.

Foreword

Games that require special venues provide new and exciting fun for its participants. The swimming pool, especially, creates a fresh and unique medium for activities of all ages. It is a distinct and matchless setting for many wholesome recreational activities involving groups of all ages, size, and diversity. Participants are benefited not only by engaging in fun activities and creating good experiences, they profit through the physical exercise as well. Activities in the swimming pool can facilitate unity and friendship, and offer a refreshing experience to its participants.

In his book, *101 Swimming Pool Games & Activities*, Jared Knight has drawn from his vast experience, knowledge, and creativity to present an impressive collection of games and activities for the swimming pool. The following 10 chapters outline activities that match a variety of circumstances; designed for individuals of all ranges in age, ability, group-size, and interest. It is very helpful that Jared has acknowledged the appropriate age range, swim level, and safety precautions for each activity. Most insightfully, a chapter has also been included that features several "back-up" activities for a rainy day or an unexpected pool closure.

This book will benefit everyone who is looking for a new and fun activity in the swimming pool. It will provide a foundation of continuous enjoyment for families and any private or public recreational group.

Kimberly Hall
Aspen Grove Family Camp

Contents

    #1: Chariot Race

    #2: Overboard

    #3: Life Jacket Race

    #4: Rubber Duck Race

    #5: Doggie Paddle Race

    #6: Underwater Race

    #7: Piggyback Race

    #8: Seaweed Race

    #9: Swimming Stroke Medley

    #10: Cannonball Contest

    #11: Swimming/Slingshot Biathlon

    #12: Ball Between the Knees Relay

    #13: Fish Eggs Relay

    #14: Seahorse Relay

    #15: Chicken Noodle Soup Relay

    #16: Beach Ball Relay

    #17: Marine Life Relay

    #18: Colander Relay

    #19: Ice Cube Relay

    #20: Umbrella Relay

    #21: Sponge Catch Relay

    #22: Blindfolded Ping-Pong Relay

Preface

Every year when I interview camp counselors for summer camp, I always ask the following question to determine if the applicant has experience in working with children and if he is able to think on his feet when dealing with children's programming. The question is: "If you were in charge of 15 eight-year-olds and you had one hour to spend with them, along with other counselors and any program equipment you desire to use, what specific game would you play?" Almost all of the answers are the same, "I would play duck, duck, goose!"

I am sure that these applicants know several other games, but with little time to prepare, this one game dominates all of the responses. More often than not, their answer reflects very little creativity and imagination. In working with children, the same dilemma often appears: It is a rainy day and the outdoor prepared programs are not available anymore, so the group has to think quickly of what to do for the next hour with 15 eight-year-olds indoors. As a manager of programs I spend a lot of time in training my staff in running games and activities, so that my camp counselors are never caught off guard and that they have numerous resources at their fingertips.

The primary purpose of *101 Swimming Pool Games & Activities* is to solve the same problem in programming—only with swimming-pool games. Almost everyone knows the game called Marco Polo. In reality, however, a number of other games exist that would also educate, entertain, and provide meaningful play for a group of children and adults for hours and hours of fun in an aquatics setting. This book provided a compendium of 101 of those games.

Introduction

The activities described in this book are fun and are designed to bring unity and team spirit to participants. They can be modified to be conducted in an indoor or nighttime setting. Furthermore, they are inexpensive and can fit most program budgets. Most of the items used for these games are already a part of the equipment supplies that are utilized in other programs by organizations such as camps and schools.

It is essential that these activities are appropriately supervised. All factors considered, keeping the swimmers engaged in organized games, activities, and events is easier to manage in an age-group environment than trying to keep track of 15 children during free-swim time. Leaders will find that more is accomplished in activities that focus on team building, strengthening self-esteem, increasing communication skills, and providing quality programs than in activities involving unstructured free-time in which children play by themselves or with one other person. This book provides simple instructions, a list of equipment needed, the recommended ages for participants, and an outline of safety precautions to aid leaders in preparing for each event.

This book is ideal for private pools owned by camps, schools, clubs, and churches, because the leaders can use the pool exclusively for games and sports. Community pools will have to be reserved in the evening or prior arrangements will have to be made with the facility's operator to conduct these games during normal pool hours. On the other hand, during busy times when a community pool is full of swimming patrons, a lifeguard may prohibit the playing of some of these games or preclude the use of some of the equipment necessary to administer the activity if he feels it is not suitable for the situation, given the larger crowd of nonparticipating swimmers. For this reason, activity leaders should make advance arrangements with pool operators and lifeguards to reserve times when the games featured in this text can be played in the community pool. In all of these games, both in private and community pools, an absolute expectation exists by the author that certified lifeguards supervise the pool and that adult activity leaders are present during the conduct of all the games.

Leaders should assess the swimming ability of each participant through a swimming test and classify participants into four categories: non-swimmer, beginning, strong, and advanced. This book details activities for individuals encompassing the entire range of skill levels—from strong/advanced to beginning/non-swimmers. One of the features of this book is a section for each game of the suggested swimming level. Creating meaningful memories in a swimming-pool setting is a key overall goal of this book. Using these games will provide leaders with both tools and ideas that can help them achieve this goal in their own aquatics programs.

1

Water World Olympics

Game #1: Chariot Race

Objective: To strengthen the leg muscles of each participant, since only the legs are used to propel the individual in the activity

Goals of Participants: To race other participants, using a kickboard

Overview: Using a kickboard, each participant swims in his lane to the opposite end of the pool and back to the starting area. The first swimmer to do this wins.

Rules: Each swimmer lies on his stomach, while holding on to the kickboard with his upper body, and moves forward, using either a whip kick or a flutter kick. Kickboards should all be uniformed, with regard to style and design.

Preparation: Leaders should set up lap lanes in the pool, with only one participant in each lane.

Number of Participants: The number of participants is determined by the number of lap lanes. If no lap lanes are available, then swimmers can either swim in a straight line or swim along the outer parameter of the pool.

Age Range and Swimming Level of Participants: Ages six and older; each participant should be able to swim independently without relying on a kickboard.

Safety Precautions: Prior to the race, each swimmer should be instructed to reposition his torso on the kickboard if his head is going under the water or if he is getting too much water in his face.

Game #2: Overboard

Objective: To teach the skill of jumping in the water feet-first, without the swimmer's head going underwater

Goals of Participants: For each participant to keep his hat from coming off as he enters the swimming pool

Overview: Each participant lines up on the deck of the swimming pool and is given a hat, such as a ball cap, to wear while jumping in the pool. Each swimmer jumps feet-first, with his legs and arms stretched out so that he does not sink too far into the water upon entry.

Rules: Any participant whose hat comes off as he jumps in the pool is out of the game. Those individuals whose hat remains on during the first round continue jumping into the pool in future rounds until other participants are eliminated and an overall winner to the game is determined.

Preparation: Leaders need a hat for each participant.

Number of Participants: Eight to 25 participants

Age Range and Swimming Level of Participants: Ages six and older; each participant should be able to swim safety back to the edge of the pool.

Safety Precautions: This jump is a standing jump that should be undertaken only from the deck of the pool—not from the diving board.

Game #3: Life Jacket Race

Objective: To increase the level of confidence and comfort for being in the pool of beginning swimmers

Goals of Participants: To race against other swimmers wearing a life jacket

Overview: Each participant is given a life jacket to wear prior to the race. When the leader says "Go," each participant floats on his back, using either a whip kick or flutter kick to float one length of the pool. The participant who reaches the opposite end of the pool first wins the race.

Rules: Swimmers should stay on their back for the entire race.

Preparation: A life jacket is needed for each swimmer. If lap lanes are available, they should be set up prior to the race.

Number of Participants: Four to six participants

Age Range and Swimming Level of Participants: Ages six and older; participants should be comfortable in swimming short distances without the use of a life jacket.

Safety Precautions: Leaders should stand at the opposite end of the pool in front of the wall. Subsequently, as the swimmers float toward the wall of the pool, leaders can prevent them from hitting the wall.

Game #4: Rubber Duck Race

Objective: To involve younger children and participants who lack the swimming skills necessary to participate in other games in the pool (It should be noted that this is a non-swimmer event that is conducted in shallow water that requires a measure of physical activity and coordination.)

Goals of Participants: To race other participants and to be the first one back to the finish area (This activity is conducted from the opposite side of the shallow-end and back to the starting area.)

Overview: While running in the shallow-end of the pool, participants each have a small rubber duck with which they have to race.

Rules: The rubber duck cannot be touched at all by participants during the race. Instead, each participant splashes water around the duck to create a current that pushes the duck to the finish area of the pool.

Preparation: A rubber duck of the same size should be provided to each participant.

Number of Participants: Eight to 12 participants

Age Range and Swimming Level of Participants: Ages six and older, including those who are non-swimmers

Safety Precautions: The playing area should be in the shallow-end of the swimming pool and large enough so that players do not trip on each other as they race.

Game #5: Doggie Paddle Race

Objective: To promote agility, coordination and the ability to do two things simultaneously

Goals of Participants: To compete with other swimmers to be the first one to complete the race, which involves performing the doggie paddle, while transporting an object

Overview: Using the doggie-paddle stroke, swimmers carry a dog-chew toy under their chin against their neck, while swimming one length of the pool.

Rules: If a swimmer drops his chew toy, he has to stop paddling and put the toy back under his chin, before continuing the race. He does not need to start the race over.

Preparation: A dog-chew toy of the same style and size must be provided to each participant

Number of Participants: Four to six swimmers

Age Range and Swimming Level of Participants: Ages 10 and older who have strong swimming skills

Safety Precautions: If a participant suffers a severe neck ache or cramp while performing this task, he should stop and release the toy from his neck and put his hands in the air. The leader should then blow a whistle to interrupt the race until that individual can readjust the toy so it is more comfortable. When the whistle blows again, all participants should restart the activity exactly where they were when they stopped initially.

Game #6: Underwater Race

Objective: To enhance the ability to swim underwater with the aid of a snorkel and mask

Goals of Participants: To swim two lengths of the pool, while competing against other swimmers

Overview: While swimming face-first with a snorkel and mask, each participant swims underwater, but close to the surface of the water for the entire course. The first participant to swim to the opposite side of the pool and back to the starting area wins the race.

Rules: Any participant who raises his head out of the water is disqualified from the race.

Preparation: Lap lanes should be set up prior to competition. A snorkel and mask should be provided to each participant. Leaders should ensure that each participant is comfortable and proficient in the use of snorkeling equipment.

Number of Participants: Four to six swimmers

Age Range and Swimming Level of Participants: Ages 12 and older who have strong swimming skills

Safety Precautions: Each participant should be cautioned prior to the race to stop swimming, raise his head out of the water, and get additional air if he is having difficulty in breathing or swallows water, or if his mask fogs up to a point where he cannot see.

Game #7: Piggyback Race

Objective: To promote teamwork by teaming adults up with younger participants to work together to finish the race

Goals of Participants: To be the first team to complete the race

Overview: The adult carries his child-teammate on his back in piggyback fashion, as each pair races toward the opposite end of the pool and back to the starting point.

Rules: The adult should have his eyes closed for the entire race, and the child riding on his back should steer the adult with verbal commands concerning which direction to go.

Preparation: Leaders set up lap lanes, and assign each team to a specific lane.

Number of Participants: Up to four two-man teams

Age Range and Swimming Level of Participants: The child-rider should be under the age of eight and should be able to swim on his own, in the event that he falls off of his adult partner's back.

Safety Precautions: Leaders should be near the edge of the pool, warning each adult when he is approaching the wall.

Game #8: Seaweed Race

Objective: To create an imaginary environment where participants pretend they are in the ocean full of seaweed as they compete in the race

Goals of Participants: To navigate through floating obstacles, while attempting to be the first one to the designated finish area

Overview: Swimmers swim to the opposite end of the pool and back without touching any of the floating seaweed particles, which are floating foam noodles.

Rules: If a participant comes in contact with a noodle, that individual has to stop swimming and count to 10 before continuing the race.

Preparation: Approximately 25 yellow foam noodles should be placed in the pool prior to the race.

Number of Participants: 10 to 15 swimmers

Age Range and Swimming Level of Participants: Ages eight and older who have strong swimming skills

Safety Precautions: Leaders should assist lifeguards in scanning the pool during the activity because all of the floating noodles at the surface of the pool could obstruct the ability to see a participant in need of assistance.

Game #9: Swimming Stroke Medley

Objective: To recognize individual achievement and the fitness level of the participants who excel in swimming

Goals of Participants: To race six lengths of the pool, using a different stroke each length

Overview: Swimmers race each other to be the first participant to swim six lengths of the pool, using all six strokes—American crawl stroke, back stroke, breast stroke, elementary back stroke, butterfly stroke, and side stroke

Rules: All participants should perform the strokes in the aforementioned order, which includes racing strokes to the opposite end of the pool, alternating with resting strokes when returning back.

Preparation: Swimming-lap lanes should be set up prior to the race; one leader should have a whistle to blow to initiate the activity.

Number of Participants: The number of participants should be determined by the number of lap lanes.

Age Range and Swimming Level of Participants: Ages 10 and older who have advanced swimming skills. Prior to the start of the race, different heats should be conducted to determine compatible competitors, based on age and swimming-skill level.

Safety Precautions: Athletes should be fit and able to complete the activity's requirements.

Game #10: Cannonball Contest

Objective: To promote coordination and skill in jumping feet-first off of the diving board

Goals of Participants: To make the biggest splash

Overview: Contestants line up at the diving board. They then jump off the diving board one at a time, tucking in their arms and legs, like a cannonball into the water below.

Rules: Five leaders serve as judges—each holding up white sheets of paper with black numbers printed on them from one to 10. The leaders evaluate the relative performance of each contestant's cannonball jump, based on how big the splash was. The winner of the contest is the participant with the highest score. Second- and third-place winners can also be recognized. Prior to the activity, a leader can make Olympic candy medals and award them to the top three finishers of this event. These medals can be made by gluing six Hershey's Kisses of the same foil color on a circle piece of card stock and attaching the card stock to a ribbon. Six gold-foil, almond Kisses make a gold medal, which is awarded to the first-place winner. In turn, six silver-foil, milk chocolate Kisses can be used to make a silver medal, which is awarded to the second-place winner. Finally, a bronze award that is awarded to the third-place winner can be made from six bronze-foil, caramel apple Kisses.

Preparation: The activity must be conducted at a swimming pool that has a diving board.

Number of Participants: 10 to 25 participants

Age Range and Swimming Level of Participants: Ages eight and older who have strong swimming skills

Safety Precautions: Participants who are jumping must wait for the previous contestant to swim to the side of the pool before jumping off of the diving board

Game #11: Swimming/Slingshot Biathlon

Objective: To apply the concept of the Winter Olympic sport of biathlon (skiing and shooting) and convert it into a game that involves swimming, while using a slingshot to aim at a target

Goals of Participants: To achieve the highest score possible by swimming with the fastest time and getting the most points in slingshot-target shooting

Overview: Using small pieces (one-inch in diameter) of a wet sponge, participants shoot the pieces of the sponge at a target, only on their first and third length laps of the pool. Each participant swims the crawl stroke and shoots the slingshot, while all of the other participants and leaders watch from the opposite side of the pool from the shooting side. The competing swimmer stands in the pool near the deck, puts on safety glasses, and retrieves the slingshot and three pieces of sponge from the deck. He then aims at an aluminum pie tin, positioned on the pool deck four feet away, that is propped up by a football kickoff tee. Every time he hits the pie tin with the sponge, he receives 10 points. After shooting, the swimmer places the slingshot back on the pool deck, swims to the opposite side of the pool, and then returns to shoot three more pieces of sponge at the pie tin. After the final round of shooting, the participant swims the final (fourth) length back and completes the race. This activity is a timed event in which, in case of a tie in the number of points earned by the target shooting, the fastest time serves as the tie-breaker. After the first swimmer completes the course, he gets out of the pool, and a second swimmer takes a turn.

Rules: When swimming, the participants swim in three to four feet of water. When shooting, the pie tin is the designated target. Participants should not aim at anything or anyone else. All participants and spectators must be at the opposite end of the pool while the activity is conducted. No one should be in the pool, but the one contestant.

Preparation: A stopwatch, a slingshot, safety glasses, a pie tin, a football kickoff tee, and six one-inch pieces of a sponge are required for the activity. The sponges should not be chemically treated.

Number of Participants: Up to six participants

Age Range and Swimming Level of Participants: Ages 12 and older who have strong swimming skills

Safety Precautions: Safety glasses should be worn by each swimmer. If the glasses fog up, participants can dip the glasses in the pool to clear them. All pieces of the sponge should be collected after the game to prevent them from getting into the pool's filtration system.

2

Swimming Relay Games

Game #12: Ball Between the Knees Relay

Objective: To combine speed with balance, as participants work in teams to complete the course

Goals of Participants: To have four-person teams compete against other teams in a relay

Overview: While running in the shallow-end of the pool during his leg of the relay, each participant goes as fast as he can to the opposite side of the shallow-end of the pool and then back, with a playground ball or beach ball between his legs.

Rules: As the first participant reaches the next runner on his team, he hands him the ball as a baton. That person then puts the ball between his legs and continues the relay. When the second runner is finished, he passes the ball to the third runner. This pattern continues until the fourth member of the team has completed the course. The team to complete the course first wins the game. In those instances where a team has participants of different ages, different sized balls may be used for each runner, instead of the same ball being passed from one team member to another.

Preparation: The size of the balls used in the activity can vary, based on the age of the participants. For example, a 10-inch playground ball can be used for adults, a seven-inch playground ball can be employed for eight-year-olds to teenagers, and a five-inch ball can be utilized for children ages five to seven.

Number of Participants: At least two teams with four participants per team

Age Range and Swimming Level of Participants: Ages six and older who have beginning swimming skills. The water should be at chest-high level for all participants. Non-swimmers can participate if they wear a life jacket.

Safety Precautions: Teams should be spaced far enough apart in order to avoid interfering with competing participants.

Game #13: Fish Eggs Relay

Objective: To increase the surface-diving skills of participants

Goals of Participants: To gather as many plastic eggs from the bottom of the swimming pool within a one-minute timeframe

Overview: One hundred plastic eggs are scattered on the bottom of the swimming pool before the activity begins. Each participant has a basket on the deck of the pool with his name on it. The basic aim of the game is to have participants collect as many eggs as they can within sixty seconds. The participant with the most eggs in his basket after one minute wins the game.

Rules: Participants can only retrieve eggs from the bottom of the pool, rather than from the baskets of other swimmers.

Preparation: Three pennies should be placed in each plastic egg to provide weight to the plastic eggs. A stopwatch is required to time the event.

Number of Participants: Five participants at a time

Age Range and Swimming Level of Participants: Ages 10 and older who have advanced swimming skills

Safety Precautions: The plastic eggs should be spread far enough apart to prevent participants from colliding with each other while retrieving the eggs.

Game #14: Seahorse Relay

Objective: To get as many individuals as possible to participate in the activity, including non-swimmers

Goals of Participants: To have each member of the five-man team perform their leg of the relay

Overview: Each participant or "cowboy" on the team runs from one side of the shallow-end of the pool and back to the starting area, while straddling a foam noodle and riding it like a "seahorse." The first team to have all five participants complete their leg of the relay wins the game.

Rules: Participants have to be on the noodle the entire course. If a participant falls off his "seahorse," he has to mount it again before he can resume competing.

Preparation: A noodle must be provided to each participant to ride on.

Number of Participants: At least two teams of five participants

Age Range and Swimming Level of Participants: Ages six and older; non-swimmers are welcome to participate in the activity.

Safety Precautions: When non-swimmers are involved in the activity, it should be conducted in chest-high water, so that participants do not rely solely on the noodle as a floatation device.

Game #15: Chicken Noodle Soup Relay

Objective: To enhance the ability of individuals to work together in order to accomplish a specific task in the shortest amount of time

Goals of Participants: To involve the entire team in gathering specified floating objects into a container, while avoiding coming in contact with another type of floating objects

Overview: Numerous yellow foam noodles and rubber chickens are placed in the pool. A team of five participants attempt to gather up all of the rubber chickens and put them in a large metal cooking pot that is positioned on the pool deck, without coming in contact with any of the floating yellow noodles. Teams compete for achieving the best time, but perform the required task one team at a time.

Rules: Anytime a team member touches a floating yellow noodle, he either has to take one of the rubber chickens out of the pot and throw it back into the center of the pool or if no rubber chickens have been collected yet, five seconds are added to the clock.

Preparation: The activity requires 25 foam noodles, 25 rubber chickens, one cooking pot, and a stopwatch.

Number of Participants: At least two teams, with five participants per team

Age Range and Swimming Level of Participants: Ages eight and older who have strong swimming skills

Safety Precautions: Competing team members should be watching from the pool deck—far enough away in order to not interfere with the participants who are actively engaged in the activity or to obstruct the opportunity of the lifeguards to see individuals in the pool.

Game #16: Beach Ball Relay

Objective: To teach cooperation to the participants

Goals of Participants: To transport a beach ball from one side of the pool and back as fast as possible

Overview: Members of two-participant teams place a beach ball between them (back to back) and race walking sideways from the opposite side of the shallow-end of the pool and back to the starting area. The team that completes the task the fastest wins the game.

Rules: The ball must be touching the back of each participant. If the ball falls from where the team is carrying it, the two team members have to return to the starting area and begin again.

Preparation: A beach ball is needed for each team.

Number of Participants: At least two two-man teams; preferably four

Age Range and Swimming Level of Participants: Ages six and older; non-swimmers can participate in the activity.

Safety Precautions: This event should be conducted in chest-high water in order to help ensure a safe environment for the youngest participants.

Game #17: Marine Life Relay

Objective: To learn about different forms of marine life

Goals of Participants: To race from one side of the swimming pool to the other side, while swimming like a different fish or type of marine life

Overview: In five-participant teams, individuals take a turn swimming to the other side and back, like a shark, marlin, sea turtle, or eel. The first team to have all participants complete the task wins the game.

Rules: As participants swim, they must be in character as a fish through the entire course.

Preparation: Prior to the activity, leaders should determine how a person swims like a shark, marlin, sea turtle, or eel and then demonstrate that information to the participants. Participants should adhere to the prescribed patterns as they swim, while simulating their assigned form of marine life.

Number of Participants: At least two five-person teams

Age Range and Swimming Level of Participants: Ages 10 and older who have strong swimming skills

Safety Precautions: Competing team members should watch the activity from the pool deck—far enough away in order to not interfere with the participants who are actively engaged in the activity or to obstruct the opportunity of the lifeguards to see individuals in the pool.

Game #18: Colander Relay

Objective: To build unity as participants work in teams to be the first group to complete the assigned task

Goals of Participants: To fill up a bucket with water

Overview: Each four-person team uses a colander to fill up a three-gallon bucket that is positioned on the deck of the swimming pool. Each participant takes a turn running to the center of the shallow-end of the pool, dipping the colander in the water, and rushing back toward the swimming pool deck.

Rules: The bucket cannot be moved from the deck during the activity. The first team to fill its bucket to its brim with water wins the game.

Preparation: A similarly sized three-gallon bucket and colander should be provided for each team.

Number of Participants: At least two teams, with four participants per team

Age Range and Swimming Level of Participants: Ages six and older; non-swimmers can participate in the activity.

Safety Precautions: The colander should be thoroughly cleansed in a dishwasher after the activity has been completed. The event should be conducted in chest-high water in order to help ensure a safe environment for the youngest participants.

Game #19: Ice Cube Relay

Objective: To teach participants that each member of the team has value and that the team cannot succeed without everyone's involvement and efforts

Goals of Participants: To swim to one side of the pool, while holding an ice cube

Overview: Prior to the race, all four team members of each team are given an ice cube that they try to keep from melting until their section of the race is completed. The first team member swims as fast as he can to the other side of the pool, where he meets the second swimmer. Holding his own ice cube, this individual races to the opposite side of the pool, where he is met by the third swimmer. This pattern continues until all four swimmers have completed their turn of the relay.

Rules: Each team participates separately and competes against the clock to determine the winner of the relay. A one-minute penalty is added to a swimmer's time if his ice cube is completely melted before he completes his leg of the relay.

Preparation: Ice cubes that are uniform in size and shape as much as possible are required for each team. For teams that are waiting their turn to participate in the activity, the ice cubes that will be given to them should be stored in a freezer or ice chest until just before the event starts for them.

Number of Participants: At least two teams, with four participants per team

Age Range and Swimming Level of Participants: Ages eight and older who have strong swimming skills

Safety Precautions: Participants should be cautioned not to hold the ice cube so tightly in their hands that pain or injury would result.

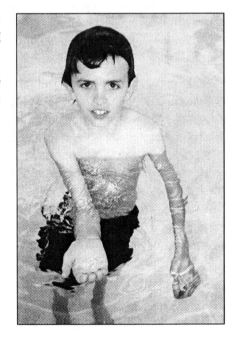

Game #20: Umbrella Relay

Objective: To serve as a nature lesson in addition to being a relay game; to provide a teambuilding opportunity for participants

Goals of Participants: To collect water to fill a bucket

Overview: One of a five-participant team stands in shallow water near the edge of the pool, holding an opened umbrella. Three other team members stand in the pool alongside the umbrella, each holding a 12-ounce plastic cup in his hands. The fifth team member is positioned on the deck, grasping a watering can. The activity commences when this participant pours water from the can over the umbrella. As the water drips off of the umbrella, the team members who are standing near the umbrella try to catch the water in their cups and dispense the water into the one-gallon bucket that is positioned on the deck.

Rules: Each team performs the required task separately. At the end of each round, a leader measures the water collected, and the team with the highest measurement wins the relay.

Preparation: An umbrella, a watering can, a one-gallon empty bucket, and a plastic 12-ounce cup for each team member are needed for the activity. The same equipment is used by each team when it is its turn.

Number of Participants: At least two teams, with five participants per team

Age Range and Swimming Level of Participants: Ages six and older; non-swimmers can participate in the activity.

Safety Precautions: Competing team members should watch the activity from the pool deck—far enough away in order to not interfere with the individuals who are actively engaged in the activity and to avoid obstructing the opportunity of the lifeguards to see participants in the pool. The activity should be conducted in chest-high water in order to help ensure a safe environment for the youngest participants.

Game #21: Sponge Catch Relay

Objective: To promote eye-hand-coordination

Goals of Participants: To work as a team in throwing and catching objects as fast as possible

Overview: Each participant on a six-member team stands in a line-formation in the shallow-part of the pool, holding a bucket full of water. The team captain, positioned at the shallow-end of the pool, has 15 wet sponges that he throws one at a time to the person behind him. That person has to catch the sponges in a bucket full of water and then throw them to the next person in line. The sponges travel in the line-formation until the last person in the line receives the sponges and sets them on the pool deck.

Rules: Participants have to stand stationary in the line-formation and to always have their buckets full of water. Any sponges that are not caught in a bucket are thrown back to the first person in line to be thrown again. This activity is a timed event. The team that transports all of the sponges from one side of the pool to the other the fastest wins the relay.

Preparation: The activity requires 15 sponges, six buckets of the same size, and a stopwatch.

Number of Participants: At least two teams, with six participants per team

Age Range and Swimming Level of Participants: Ages six and older; non-swimmers can participate in the activity.

Safety Precautions: The activity should be conducted in chest-high water to help ensure a safe environment for the youngest participants. Only sponges that have not been chemically treated should be used.

Game #22: Blindfolded Ping-Pong Relay

Objective: To develop trust in receiving directions and advice given by fellow team members

Goals of Participants: To gather up as many ping-pong balls as possible in the shortest amount of time

Overview: Using a funnel made from an old beach towel that has a hole in the center, each six-member team attempts to first find 25 ping-pong balls that are floating in the pool and then drop them in the funnel. The balls are sent through the funnel (held by two members of the team) to a bucket that is held by another designated team member (i.e., the team leader). The team members who are gathering the floating balls are blindfolded. The team leader, along with the two individuals who are holding the ends of the funnel, can see, but they cannot move from their stations. These three team members must coach their blindfolded teammates to find all of the balls and to direct them toward the funnel.

Rules: All ping pong-balls must be sent through the funnel, rather than just being gathered into the bucket. This activity is a timed event in which each team performs the required task separately. The team that achieves the highest score (i.e., the most balls funneled into the bucket) wins the game.

Preparation: The activity requires 25 ping-pong balls, a beach towel, a small bucket, three blindfolds, and a stopwatch.

Number of Participants: At least two teams, with six participants per team

Age Range and Swimming Level of Participants: Ages eight and older who have strong swimming skills

Safety Precautions: The activity should be conducted in the shallow-end of the swimming pool. Participants who are gathering the ping-pong balls should be good swimmers because they engage in the task while blindfolded. Someone should also be positioned in the pool to gather those ping-pong balls that float into the deeper end of the swimming pool. This individual should also be ready to assist any blindfolded participants who become disoriented.

3

Waterworks Games

Game #23: Bouncing Bubbles

Objective: To provide an activity that people who are just arriving at the pool can play, while they wait for other individuals to arrive

Goals of Participants: To launch as many bouncy balls as possible into a floating basket that is positioned in the center of the pool within a 30-second timeframe

Overview: Each participant stands on the swimming pool deck and bounces a small bouncy ball one at a time off the surface of the deck.

Rules: One point is awarded to each participant for each ball that lands in the floating basket. The participant with the most points wins the game.

Preparation: The activity requires 25 bouncy balls, a laundry basket that floats (if the basket cannot float, it can be placed on a kickboard), and a stopwatch.

Number of Participants: Up to five people at a time

Age Range and Swimming Level of Participants: Ages six and older; non-swimmers can also participate in the activity as long as it is conducted in the shallow-end of the swimming pool and that children under the age of 10 who do not swim wear life jackets.

Safety Precautions: Participants and spectators should not run on the deck of the pool and should use caution while standing near the water.

Game #24: Dodge Beach Ball

Objective: To promote physical exercise and provide an opportunity to engage in competition that is fun

Goals of Participants: To avoid getting hit by the ball and being eliminated from the game

Overview: Two six-member teams face each other and determine a line at which each team cannot cross into the other team's territory. When the game begins, participants throw beach balls at their opponents to hit them and eliminate them from the game. To dodge an incoming thrown ball, participants can move from side to side and even go under water and resurface seconds later. If anyone gets hit with the ball, he is out of the game. If a participant throws a ball at an opponent and the opponent catches the ball, the participant who threw the ball is out of the game.

Rules: Participants should only aim at their opponent's arms, shoulders, and back area and not at either the head or neck area. This activity should be conducted in shallow water.

Preparation: The activity requires 10 large beach balls that are shared by both teams.

Number of Participants: Two teams, with six players per team

Age Range and Swimming Level of Participants: Ages 12 and older who have strong swimming skills

Safety Precautions: Participants should be cautioned prior to the activity to stand away from the steps and pool walls to avoid possibly being injured by contact with the hard surfaces. Individuals should also spread out far enough from their teammates in order to keep from colliding with each other as they attempt to avoid incoming thrown balls.

Game #25: Pool in the Pool

Objective: To provide an opportunity to play an adapted game of "eight-ball" pool on the bottom of a zero-entry or wading pool

Goals of Participants: To roll a cue ball in an attempt to hit seven pool balls positioned on the bottom of the swimming pool toward the numbered spots before a competing participant does

Overview: Six vinyl spots, numbered one to six, are placed on the floor of the swimming pool. Each player takes a turn softly rolling a cue ball toward the seven balls, aiming at the vinyl spots. On each attempt, if the player makes his ball land on the numbered spot, he can continue playing. Otherwise, it is his opponent's turn who resumes play where the first player left off. This activity works best in either a zero entry-pool or a wading pool that has a gradual slope.

Rules: The rules of "eight-ball" pool are modified by having one participant play the striped balls and the other participant play the solid balls. Neither player can get the cue ball or the eight ball on a spot without being penalized. If the eight ball lands on the spot, then the game is over, and the other player automatically wins. If the cue ball lands on a spot, it is called a "scratch," and the cue ball is given to the other player, who can place it on the pool floor where he wants it for his turn.

Preparation: Six vinyl spots with numbers should be lined up so that three spots are in two rows adjacent from each other, similar to a pool table. The distance in which the spots are positioned should be determined by the playing space available. The activity requires 15 pool balls.

Number of Participants: Two participants

Age Range and Swimming Level of Participants: Ages five and older; this activity is designed for young children and non-swimmers.

Safety Precautions: Participants must be aware of where all of the balls are so they do not stumble and trip over the balls. Participants should also avoid standing on the vinyl spots.

Game #26: Target Ball

Objective: To develop patience and skill through practice

Goals of Participants: To roll a ball into a floating basket

Overview: Each participant takes a turn rolling an eight-inch playground ball down a pool slide into a floating laundry basket that is positioned in the pool at the base of the slide.

Rules: Each player has three turns to roll his ball down the slide. He gets one point for every time the ball lands in the basket. The player who earns the most points wins the game.

Preparation: The activity requires a laundry basket that floats or can float on a kickboard and three eight-inch playground balls.

Number of Participants: Up to 10 participants

Age Range and Swimming Level of Participants: Ages five and older; this activity is designed for young children and non-swimmers. An activity leader should be in the pool to retrieve the balls.

Safety Precautions: All participants should line up in a single file line at the slide, where they can be readily observed by the lifeguards. No participant should slide down the pool slide during this activity.

Game #27: Splash Out

Objective: To practice performing a specific skill in the fastest time possible

Goals of Participants: To extinguish a candle with water from the swimming pool

Overview: A small candle is positioned on the pool deck, and each participant stands in chest-high water in the swimming pool. With a squirt gun, each individual takes a turn attempting to squirt out the flame of the candle. The activity is a timed event. The participant with the fastest time wins the game.

Rules: The candle is placed three feet away from the participant on the pool deck, who must be stationary as he attempts to extinguish the flame.

Preparation: The activity requires matches, a squirt gun, a stopwatch, and a candle.

Number of Participants: Up to 10 players

Age Range and Swimming Level of Participants: Ages eight and older; non-swimmers can participate in the activity.

Safety Precautions: The candle and its wax must not be allowed to go into the pool. Only an adult leader should be near the candle, and that person must remain near the candle the entire time in order to keep the candle from becoming a tripping hazard for the other participants.

Game #28: Pocket Quest

Objective: To provide a way to motivate children to leave the pool and to gather up their belongings in a fun way at the end of the swimming day

Goals of Participants: To win a scavenger hunt

Overview: The activity involves a "boys-versus-girls" competition in which at the end of the swim time after children get back into their street clothes, boys and girls collect designated belongings of their teammates, such as a blue sock, a family photo, a silver belt buckle, a shoelace, a key chain, sunscreen, a dime, a flip flop, a comb, a rubber band, etc. After everyone is dressed and leaves the locker room, the two teams start collecting the designated items, under adult supervision. For each item collected on the list, five points are awarded to the team.

Rules: The activity officially starts after everyone is dressed in his street clothes and is outside of the locker room. Participants cannot collect items without getting permission to acquire the item first, a stipulation that should eliminate participants from collecting lost and found-type items or going back into the locker room and randomly looking through vacant lockers.

Preparation: The activity requires a list of items that both a boy and a girl might reasonably have in their pockets or on their person.

Number of Participants: Two teams of up to 20 people per team

Age Range and Swimming Level of Participants: Ages five and older; this game can include non-swimmers.

Safety Precautions: Prior to this activity commencing, participants should be cautioned not to use verbal or physical force to bully others to obtain their personal belongings without their consent. Participants should be warned that any such behavior will automatically disqualify the team from the game. Steps should be taken to ensure that all belongings are returned to their rightful owners after the game concludes.

Game #29: Floating Pyramid

Objective: To promote teamwork; to enhance coordination

Goals of Participants: To try to float in a pyramid formation

Overview: Each team member floats on his back and tries to coordinate with the other two members of his team to form a pyramid. A leader, who is standing on the pool deck, judges each team on how well a pyramid is formed.

Rules: Participants should not hold hands. Rather, they should have their arms stretched out, touching the arms of their teammates on both sides.

Preparation: A leader should award points on a scale from one to 10, with the number 10 being the highest. After each team performs, the leader should note the number achieved by each team on a sheet of paper with a marker.

Number of Participants: At least two teams of three participants

Age Range and Swimming Level of Participants: Ages 10 and older who have advanced swimming skills; beginning swimmers can participate in the activity if they wear life jackets.

Safety Precautions: Only swimmers who are comfortable floating should be allowed to participate in the activity. Other individuals should not exert pressure on their teammates who cannot perform the required task, once the activity has started.

Game #30: Sharks, Octopuses, and Eels

Objective: To teach about the food chain

Goals of Participants: To produce a greater hand-sign than the opponent

Overview: Two people line up facing each other in the shallow-end of the swimming pool. On the count of three, both participants go completely under the water and resurface, exhibiting a shark, octopus, or eel hand-sign. Depending on the hand-sign used by each participant, a winner is determined for each round of the game. Because a shark can eat an eel, a shark hand-sign wins over an eel hand-sign. In turn, since an octopus can eat a shark, an octopus hand-sign wins over a shark hand-sign. Furthermore, because an eel can eat an octopus, an eel hand-sign wins over an octopus hand-sign.

Rules: To make the shark hand-sign, a participant places one of his hands on his head so it looks like a shark fin. To make the octopus hand-sign, a participant moves his fingers up and down on his right hand to look like an octopus swimming. To make the eel hand-sign, a participant waves his right hand back and forth like a snake.

Preparation: Players should agree on the aforementioned hand-signs prior to the game.

Number of Participants: Two participants

Age Range and Swimming Level of Participants: Ages six and older; non-swimmers can participate in the activity if the game is conducted in the shallow-end of the swimming pool.

Safety Precautions: The game should be conducted in an open area of the pool away from other swimmers.

4

Water Carnival

Game #31: Apple Catch

Objective: To provide a fun-filled activity; to promote hand-eye coordination

Goals of Participants: To gather as many apples as possible within a specified timeframe

Overview: The activity involves a new twist on a traditional Halloween game called Bobbing for Apples. Instead of biting the apple, each participant is in the pool and is required to collect as many floating apples as possible, using a fork, within a 30-second timeframe. The game is conducted individually for a prize that is given at the end of the carnival, after the participants have left the pool area. The game is conducted in the shallow-end of the swimming pool where each participant (one at a time) tries to spear a floating apple, using only a fork. Once the apple is on the fork, the participant walks toward a three-gallon bucket that is positioned on the swimming pool deck and places the apple in the bucket.

Rules: A five-apple penalty (i.e., five apples are not counted in the final total) is given to a participant if pieces break off of any of the apples while they are being collected. The ideal situation is not to have any broken pieces of the apples floating in the pool to clog the filtration system. To win the game, a minimum of 10 apples must be collected, a number that can vary, based on the age of the participants.

Preparation: The activity requires a predetermined number of apples (e.g., 25) for each participant. Apples can subsequently be used again if they are still in good shape. The game also requires a whistle and a stopwatch. At the end of the carnival, each participant receives a plastic lace necklace. If a participant wins the game, he receives a different colored pony bead as the prize. For the game "apple catch," the suggested bead color is red.

Number of Participants: Up to 20 players

Age Range and Swimming Level of Participants: Ages six and older; non-swimmers can participate in the activity.

Safety Precautions: An adult leader should be in the pool to retrieve apples that have drifted into the deeper section of the pool. Participants should use caution when using a fork while attempting to gather apples in order to prevent injuries. Individuals who are currently not actively participating in the contest should not be in the activity area during the game. The water should be chest-high for all participants.

Game #32: Hoop Ball

Objective: To develop persistence and skill in throwing a ball

Goals of Participants: To throw a playground ball into a hoop that is seven feet away

Overview: A participant has to throw the ball through the hoop 10 times in a row to win the game. The hoop is held by another participant who is standing seven feet away. The activity is done individually, and a prize is given to the game's winner at the end of the carnival, after the participants have left the pool area.

Rules: The hoop is held in a vertical position in the shallow-end of the swimming pool. Both the thrower and the hoop should be stationary during the game.

Preparation: The activity requires a 24-inch hoop and a playground ball. At the end of the carnival, each participant receives a plastic lace necklace. If a participant wins the game, he receives a different colored pony bead as the prize. For the game "hoop ball," the suggested bead color is blue.

Number of Participants: Up to 20 players

Age Range and Swimming Level of Participants: Ages six and older; non-swimmers can participate in the activity.

Safety Precautions: The person holding the hoop should be alert during the game in order to avoid being hit by the ball. The water should be chest-high for all participants.

Game #33: Peach Fling

Objective: To highlight the origin of the game of basketball, which initially involved throwing a ball into a peach basket

Goals of Participants: To toss plastic peaches into a floating peach basket that is floating in the center of the swimming pool

Overview: Each participant is given 10 plastic peaches to toss into the basket. He must make seven baskets in order to win the game and receive a prize. The activity is done individually, and a prize is given at the end of the carnival, after the participants have left the pool area.

Rules: The peach basket is floating on a kickboard. Because the basket is floating, it will move slightly on the water. The participant, however, must stand stationary in his original spot, where he must adjust each toss with the current location of the peach basket.

Preparation: The activity requires a kickboard, a peach basket, and 10 plastic peaches. At the end of the carnival, each participant receives a plastic lace necklace. If the participant wins the game, he receives a different colored pony bead as the prize. For the game "peach fling," the suggested bead color is orange.

Number of Participants: Up to 20 players

Age Range and Swimming Level of Participants: Ages six and older; non-swimmers can participate in the activity.

Safety Precautions: Small children should be cautioned that the peaches used in the game are made of plastic.

Game #34: Soda Can Pitch

Objective: To promote skill and agility in throwing an object toward a target

Goals of Participants: To knock down a stack of six empty soda cans, using a wet sponge

Overview: Six soda cans are placed one on top of each other in a pyramid fashion on the deck of the swimming pool. Each participant has five turns to knock down the stack with a sponge to win a prize. The activity is done individually, and a prize is awarded at the end of the carnival, after the participants have left the pool area.

Rules: Each participant stands six feet away from the edge of the pool in the shallow-end.

Preparation: The activity requires six empty soda cans and a wet sponge. The sponge should not be chemically treated. At the end of the carnival, each participant receives a plastic lace necklace. If a participant wins the game, he receives a different colored pony bead as the prize. For the game "soda can pitch," the suggested bead color is green.

Number of Participants: Up to 20 players

Age Range and Swimming Level of Participants: Ages six and older; non-swimmers can participate in the activity.

Safety Precautions: The cans should be empty and should be rinsed out with water to prevent a slipping hazard on the pool deck.

Game #35: Ping-Pong Ball Toss

Objective: To test the skill and patience of participants, given that the designated targets get progressively more difficult to hit with each throw

Goals of Participants: To throw ping-pong balls in floating hoops to earn points

Overview: Participants throw 10 ping-pong balls toward five different hoops that are positioned in the water. The activity is done individually for a prize that is given at the end of the carnival, after the participants have left the pool area.

Rules: Each hoop is worth different points. The hoop that is the nearest to the participant is 10 points, while the hoop that is floating the farthest away is 50 points. Participants need a minimum of 100 points to win a prize.

Preparation: The activity requires five 24-inch hoops and 10 ping-pong balls. At the end of the carnival, each participant receives a plastic lace necklace. If a participant wins the game, he receives a different colored pony bead as the prize. For the game "ping-pong ball toss," the suggested bead color is white.

Number of Participants: Up to 20 players

Age Range and Swimming Level of Participants: Ages six and older; non-swimmers can participate in the activity.

Safety Precautions: The game should be played in shallow-water. An activity leader should be positioned in the pool to retrieve ping-pong balls that drift to the deep-section of the pool.

Game #36: Ring Toss

Objective: To increase eye-hand coordination

Goals of Participants: To toss plastic rings onto plastic water bottles for points

Overview: Each participant stands in chest-high water in the swimming pool, five feet from the pool deck, and tosses plastic rings at 10 plastic water bottles. For each water bottle that a ring lands on, the participant gets one point. Participants need at least five points to win a prize.

Rules: The water bottles are positioned on the pool deck, one foot away from the edge of the water. The participant must stand in the same spot to throw all 10 rings.

Preparation: The activity requires 10 plastic 12-ounce water bottles that are full of water and 10 plastic rings. At the end of the carnival, each participant receives a plastic lace necklace. If a participant wins the game, he receives a different colored pony bead as the prize. For the game "ring toss," the suggested bead color is yellow.

Number of Participants: Up to 20 players

Age Range and Swimming Level of Participants: Ages six and older; non-swimmers can participate in the activity.

Safety Precautions: The activity should be played away from other participants in order to avoid possible injuries.

Game #37: Frisbee Knock

Objective: To develop the ability to coordinate speed with accuracy in an attempt to perform a task

Goals of Participants: To knock down as many cones with a Frisbee as possible in a 30-second timeframe

Overview: Each participant stands in chest-high water, five feet away from the pool deck, where 12 cones are lined up. Each cone is worth one point. To win the game, participants need six points.

Rules: Participants have to stand stationary during the entire game.

Preparation: The activity requires 12 cones, a stopwatch, and up to 25 Frisbees. At the end of the carnival, each participant receives a plastic lace necklace. If a player wins the game, he receives a different colored pony bead as the prize. For the game "Frisbee knock," the suggested bead color is purple.

Number of Participants: Up to 20 players

Age Range and Swimming Level of Participants: Ages six and older; non-swimmers can participate in the activity.

Safety Precautions: The activity should be played away from other participants in order to avoid possible injuries caused by flying Frisbees.

Game #38: Garbage Can Ball

Objective: To practice coordinating efforts to perform a specific task

Goals of Participants: To gather floating tennis balls and carefully throw them into a clean plastic garbage can

Overview: One to three participants are positioned in the swimming pool, attempting to collect floating tennis balls and throw them gently into a garbage can. Another member of the team is positioned on the pool deck, tipping the garbage can at an angle so the balls can be more easily thrown into the can. The team has 45 seconds to gather as many balls as possible and softly toss them into the garbage can. If the team collects at least 10 balls, each member of the team receives a prize.

Rules: If the throwing participants miss the can completely, the individual holding the garbage can cannot retrieve that ball; he must stand stationary throughout the game. All balls cannot be thrown farther than three feet away from the garbage can.

Preparation: The activity requires 25 new tennis balls, a stopwatch, and a clean plastic garbage can. At the end of the carnival, each participant receives a plastic lace necklace. If a participant wins the game, he receives a different colored pony bead as the prize. For the game "garbage can ball," the suggested bead color is grey.

Number of Participants: Teams of two to four players at a time perform; up to 10 teams can participate in the activity—one at a time.

Age Range and Swimming Level of Participants: Ages 10 and older who are strong swimmers

Safety Precautions: The game should be conducted in an area that is separated from other swimmers and does not obstruct the opportunity of the lifeguard to see participants in the water.

Game #39: Lucky Duck

Objective: To involve smaller children in an activity in which they can learn number recognition

Goals of Participants: To find a lucky duck

Overview: In an either zero-entry pool or a wading pool, small children pick up a rubber duck to see if the #1 is on the bottom of the duck. Participants who find the #1 on the bottom of the duck get a point. Once a participant has five points, he receives several fish-type crackers that he can eat after the activity has finished.

Rules: All of the ducks that do not have the #1 on their bottom will have the #2. If a child finds a duck with #2 on it, he must put it back in the water and keep looking for a duck with #1. Of the 20 ducks in the wading pool, five of them should have #1 written on their bottom, while the rest should have #2.

Preparation: The activity requires 20 rubber ducks and a permanent marker.

Number of Participants: Five participants at a time, up to 20 participants total

Age Range and Swimming Level of Participants: Ages three to five; the activity is particularly designed for non-swimmers.

Safety Precautions: For toddlers, the water should be shallow—approximately a foot to two feet maximum. The adult-to-children ratio for the activity should be one child participant to one adult leader.

Game #40: Egg Walk

Objective: To encourage the use of balance and patience

Goals of Participants: To catch a floating plastic egg with a spoon and transport it, using that spoon, to the opposite side of the pool

Overview: The participants are in chest-high water. Each participant identifies a plastic egg from several eggs that are floating on the water's surface and scoops it up, using his spoon and one of his hands. The participant must use his spoon, rather than just picking the egg up and placing it on the spoon. After the egg is on the spoon, the participant walks carrying the egg, without touching it with his hands.

Rules: If the egg falls off while being transported, the participant must start over from the beginning area. If the egg can be gathered on the spoon and carried to the other end of the swimming pool in a minute or less, the participant wins a prize.

Preparation: The activity requires at least 10 large plastic eggs, one large spoon, and a stopwatch. At the end of the carnival, each participant receives a plastic lace necklace. If a player wins the game, he receives a different colored pony bead as the prize. For the game "egg walk," the suggested bead color is pink.

Number of Participants: Up to four players at a time

Age Range and Swimming Level of Participants: Ages six and older; non-swimmers can participate in the activity.

Safety Precautions: An adult leader should be in the pool gathering eggs that have drifted into the deep-end of the pool.

Game #41: Submarine Race

Objective: To teach accountability and balance

Goals of Participants: To race against the clock to get six submarines from the starting area to the finish line at the opposite side of the pool within a one-minute timeframe.

Overview: In the shallow-end of the pool, each participant has six plastic kazoos or "submarines" that he cannot touch with his hands. The game involves having the participant create waves with his hands that move all six "submarines" at the same time from one side of the pool toward the opposite side. Participants must keep track of the six objects and complete another task in a designated time. At the end of the race, all six items have to be accounted for.

Rules: All six "submarines" have to cross the finish line within the one-minute deadline in order for the participant to receive a prize.

Preparation: The activity requires six plastic kazoos and a stopwatch. At the end of the carnival, each participant receives a plastic lace necklace. If a participant wins the game, he receives a different colored pony bead as the prize. For the game "submarine race," the suggested bead color is black.

Number of Participants: Up to 20 players

Age Range and Swimming Level of Participants: Ages six and older; non-swimmers can participate in the activity.

Safety Precautions: An adult leader should be in the pool, gathering kazoos that have drifted into the deep-end of the pool. The activity should be conducted in chest-high water in order to enable non-swimmers to participate in the game.

Game #42: Water Carousel

Objective: To promote listening and attentive skills

Goals of Participants: To compete against other individuals, as everyone walks in a circle while music is playing; when the music stops, all participants must stand on the nearest spot on the floor

Overview: The pool floor has six vinyl spots that are positioned in a large circle. Each spot has a number on it from one to six. A group of six participants starts off the game by standing on a vinyl spot. Music is then played from either the pool's sound system or a nearby music-playing device. In the game, each person advances clockwise around the circle, walking on each spot. When the music stops, participants advance forward to the nearest spot. The activity leader then calls out a number from one to six. The participant who is standing on that number gets one point. Several rounds of the game are then played. Once a player earns five points total, he receives a prize.

Rules: Only one person can stand on a spot at a time.

Preparation: The activity requires six vinyl spots, with each spot labeled with a number from one to six, a music CD, and a CD player. At the end of the carnival, each participant receives a plastic lace necklace. If a participant wins the game, he receives a different colored pony bead as the prize. For the game "water carousel," the suggested bead color is brown.

Number of Participants: Six participants

Age Range and Swimming Level of Participants: Ages six and older; non-swimmers can participate in the activity.

Safety Precautions: Each participant should be warned in advance that he should use caution when he steps on each of the vinyl spots, in case the spot moves slightly under his weight. All non-swimmers should wear a life jacket. The activity should be conducted in chest-high water so that non-swimmers can participate in the game.

5

Swimming Pool Sports

Game #43: Water Football

Objective: To adapt the game of football into a swimming-pool setting to provide an opportunity for exercise and physical activity

Goals of Participants: To play football in the shallow-section of the pool

Overview: The activity involves both running and passing. The offensive team attempts to advance to their end zone, which is determined by both teams prior to the game, while the defensive team tries to stop the offensive team from advancing the football. The ball advances either by completing short passes or by running the ball. Opponents touch the shoulders or upper arms of players who have the football to stop the play. Participants should not tackle or dunk players underwater in order to get the ball.

Rules: The offensive team is given four attempts to get the ball into their end zone. The game does not award first downs for advancing the ball, because it is difficult to accurately measure distances. After four attempts, if the offensive team hasn't reached its end zone, the defensive team takes the ball at the spot at which it was last played.

Preparation: The activity requires a football and a whistle for two adult leaders.

Number of Participants: Two teams of five players per team

Age Range and Swimming Level of Participants: Ages 12 and older who have strong swimming skills

Safety Precautions: Adult leaders should referee the game to encourage safety and good sportsmanship. All participants, spectators, and referees should follow the commands and directions of the supervising lifeguard(s).

Game #44: Water Basketball

Objective: To promote teamwork by playing an adapted game of basketball in the swimming pool

Goals of Participants: To win the game

Overview: Because of limited space in the pool, both teams use the same rim/backboard that is positioned on the pool deck when they have the ball. Each made basket counts for two points. The two teams decide on how long the game lasts. For example, the first team to earn 20 points could be designated the winner.

Rules: Unlike the traditional game of basketball, participants do not dribble the ball as they move toward the basketball rim. Rather, the game involves passing the ball among team members, before subsequently shooting it in an attempt to score.

Preparation: The activity requires a rubber basketball, whistles for two adult leaders, and a basketball rim/backboard.

Number of Participants: Two teams of five players

Age Range and Swimming Level of Participants: Ages 12 and older who have good swimming skills

Safety Precautions: Two adult leaders should referee the game in order to encourage safety and good sportsmanship. All participants, spectators, and referees should follow the commands and directions of the supervising lifeguard(s).

Game #45: Punch Ball

Objective: To adapt the game of kickball in a water setting to encourage creativity and imagination

Goals of Participants: To accumulate more points than the opposing team

Overview: Two five-member teams compete against each other. One team is in the outfield (i.e., on the opposite side of the pool from the hitter), standing along the three bases. The other team attempts to score by having each member of the team punch a medium-sized playground ball with his fist toward the outfield. When the ball is punched, the hitter of the ball then runs the three bases and returns to home plate, where he first hit the ball. If a member of the opposing team catches the ball before it touches the water, the hitter of the ball is out.

Rules: The team that is trying to score can continue hitting the ball and advancing the bases until team members get three outs. At that point, the opposing team trades places with the team on offense and tries to score. In order to get a runner out with the ball, the ball cannot be thrown at the runner; instead, the runner has to be tagged with the ball. Nine innings of the game are played. At the end of the ninth inning, the team with the highest score wins the game.

Preparation: The activity requires four vinyl spots for the bases and a playground ball.

Number of Participants: Two teams of five players

Age Range and Swimming Level of Participants: Ages 12 and older who have strong swimming skills

Safety Precautions: Participants should be warned not to run onto the bases (the vinyl spots) in order to prevent the bases from slipping on the pool's floor. A runner should only stand on the base after he has reached the base and has come to a complete stop. Three adult activity leaders should referee the game to encourage safety and good sportsmanship. All participants, spectators, and referees should follow the commands and directions of the supervising lifeguard(s).

Game #46: Water Baseball

Objective: To adapt the game of baseball to encourage cooperation and team spirit

Goals of Participants: To accumulate more points than the opposing team

Overview: Two five-person teams compete against each other. One team is positioned in the outfield (the opposite side of the pool from the batter), standing along the three bases. The other team attempts to score by having each member of the team take turns hitting a ball that is pitched to them with a plastic bat. When the ball is hit, the participant runs the three bases and returns to home plate, where he first hit the ball. If a member of the opposing team catches the ball before it touches the water, the batter is out.

Rules: The team that is trying to score can continue hitting the ball and advancing the bases until team members get three outs. At that point, the opposing team trades places with the offensive team and tries to score. The runner has to be tagged with the ball in order to be out. The pitcher from the other team can try to strike out the batter (i.e., three strikes). Any ball that is hit out of the swimming pool is considered an automatic homerun. Nine innings of the game are played. At the end of the ninth inning, the team with the highest score wins the game.

Preparation: The activity requires a plastic bat, a plastic ball, and four vinyl spots for the bases.

Number of Participants: Two teams of five players

Age Range and Swimming Level of Participants: Ages 12 and older who have strong swimming skills

Safety Precautions: Participants should be warned not to run onto the bases (the vinyl spots) to prevent the bases from slipping on the pool's floor. A runner should only stand on the base after he has reached the base and has come to a complete stop. Three adult activity leaders should referee the game to encourage safety and good sportsmanship. All participants, spectators, and referees should follow the commands and directions of the supervising lifeguard(s).

Game #47: Water Volleyball

Objective: To participate in an adapted version of the game of volleyball

Goals of Participants: To try to get more points than the competition

Overview: A pennant string is hung several feet above the water's surface in the shallow-end of the swimming pool prior to the game to serve as the net. One team at a time serves a volleyball over the pennant string in an attempt to score. The serving team scores if the other team cannot return the ball back over the net in three hits or less. The ball cannot touch the water. If it does, the serving team scores a point. If the receiving team returns the ball by hitting it over the net, then the serving team has to get it back over the net in three hits or less, without the ball touching the water. If the serving team fails to do this, the opposing team then becomes the serving team.

Rules: Both teams should decide in advance the boundaries of the volleyball court in order to determine what constitutes the ball being out of bounds.

Preparation: The activity requires pennant string and a volleyball.

Number of Participants: Two teams of five players

Age Range and Swimming Level of Participants: Ages 12 and older who have strong swimming skills.

Safety Precautions: All participants, spectators, and referees should follow the commands and directions of the supervising lifeguard(s).

Game #48: Water Ping-Pong

Objective: To teach ingenuity to participants by adapting a table-top game to be played in four-feet of water, without a table

Goals of Participants: To keep the ping pong-ball on the participant's side from hitting the water

Overview: Two teams of two participants per team stand in a line in the shallow-end of the swimming pool, facing each other, with a four-foot gap between the two teams. Each person has a ping-pong paddle in his hand. Participants on the same side of the line are on the same team. One team (the serving team) starts the game by hitting the ball across to any member of the other team. A member of that team (the receiving team) must return the ball back to the serving team, without the ball touching the water. If the ball touches the water, the serving team receives a point. If the serving team cannot subsequently return the ball back to the receiving team, the receiving team then becomes the serving team.

Rules: Only the serving team can earn points. The first team to reach 10 points with a two-point lead over the other team wins the game.

Preparation: The activity requires four ping-pong paddles and one ping-pong ball.

Number of Participants: Two teams of two players

Age Range and Swimming Level of Participants: Ages 10 and older; non-swimmers can participate in the activity.

Safety Precautions: Adult activity leaders should assist participants by retrieving the ball if it drifts into the deeper end of the pool. All participants, spectators, and referees should follow the commands and directions of the supervising lifeguard(s).

Game #49: Water Polo

Objective: To encourage team play, good sportsmanship, and exercise

Goals of Participants: To win the game by earning the most points by getting the ball into the other team's goal, while simultaneously defending their own goal

Overview: Two seven-player teams compete against each other. Two goals are located on opposite sides of the pool on the two decks. One member of each team serves as his team's goalkeeper to defend the team's goal. The ball is passed among offensive players, attempting to advance it toward the goal. The team with the ball has 35 seconds to score by getting the ball into the defensive team's goal. If it is unable to do so, the possession of the ball transfers to the other team. The team that is defending their goal and guarding offensive players can employ either a man-to-man defensive strategy (one player guarding only one opponent) or a zone-defensive strategy (one player guarding a specific area). The team with the most points at the end of the four quarters of time (each quarter lasts approximately 12 minutes) wins the game.

Rules: Fouls are penalties assessed for excessively grabbing the ball, or for pushing, kicking, or exhibiting aggressive behavior. Two adult referees, each with a whistle to stop the game, if necessary, should be in the water to transfer the ball to the other team when a foul occurs. The referees should make as many penalty calls as needed to encourage safety and good sportsmanship among team members.

Preparation: The activity requires a water polo ball or a volleyball, two goals, a stopwatch for the timekeeper, and two whistles for the adult referees.

Number of Participants: Two teams of seven players

Age Range and Swimming Level of Participants: Ages 12 and older who have strong swimming skills

Safety Precautions: All participants, spectators, and referees should follow the commands and directions of the supervising lifeguard(s).

Game #50: Touchdown

Objective: To enhance sportsmanship and emphasize positive assertiveness

Goals of Participants: To stand in the swimming pool's end zone and catch a touchdown pass

Overview: One player serves as the quarterback, who throws the football into the designated end zone, where four other participants are standing, waiting to catch the football. The player who catches the ball receives a point. When one individual earns five points, he trades places with the quarterback.

Rules: Prior to the game, activity leaders give the following instructions, which should also be enforced during the game: no pushing, shoving, or stripping a ball from other players; participants can block a pass only when the ball is still in the air in an attempt to catch it themselves.

Preparation: The activity requires a football.

Number of Participants: Five players

Age Range and Swimming Level of Participants: Ages 12 and older who have strong swimming skills

Safety Precautions: All participants should follow the commands and directions of the supervising lifeguard(s).

Game #51: End Zone Frisbee

Objective: To adapt the game of Ultimate Frisbee to a smaller playing area in the swimming pool; to encourage fair competition and fun

Goals of Participants: To gain more points than the opposing team

Overview: This game involves both teams using only one end zone area, as a half-court game of Ultimate Frisbee is played. The end zone is set off with four orange cones that are set on the deck of the shallow-end of the swimming pool. The starting area is on the opposite side of the end zone. The activity is only a passing game, in which no one can run once he has received the Frisbee. If the Frisbee is intercepted by the other team or is not caught by the team that is currently throwing the Frisbee, then the opposite team takes procession of the Frisbee and walks it back to starting area to begin passing it toward the end zone. One point is awarded each time the offensive team catches a Frisbee in the end zone. The first team to score to 10 wins the game.

Rules: Once an offensive player has caught the Frisbee, he can only move up to three steps to stop his momentum. At that point, he has to stand stationary as he throws the Frisbee. The defensive players who guard the offensive team must stand three feet away and cannot come in contact with any player who throws the Frisbee, a provision that precludes stripping the Frisbee out of a player's hands.

Preparation: The activity requires four cones, two whistles for the referees, and a Frisbee.

Number of Participants: Two teams of four players

Age Range and Swimming Level of Participants: Ages 12 and older who have strong swimming skills.

Safety Precautions: The bottom of the end zone should be at least six feet from the pool wall to avoid possible injuries. Two adult activity leaders should referee the game to encourage safety and good sportsmanship. All participants, spectators, and referees should follow the commands and directions of the supervising lifeguard(s).

Game #52: Beach Ball Foosball

Objective: To illustrate the importance of how collaboration among partnerships can benefit a larger team effort

Goals of Participants: To attempt to move the ball toward the opposing team's goal

Overview: Two nine-member teams face each other in four alternating rows, with four people standing side by side in a row (similar to a foosball-table line formation). Two opposing goalies at both ends of the playing area guard the goals, which are either orange cones or plastic/net goals. Using their hands, the offensive team tries to fling the beach ball over the heads of the defensive participants and onto another row of offensive players, who catch it. The offensive team continues this process until the ball reaches the defensive team's goal. The team that is defending its goal can also try to block offensive passes in an attempt to take over the possession of the ball. The goalies try to catch the ball and toss it back into the foosball court.

Rules: Defensive and offensive players can only move from side-to-side, rather than from front-to-back, like in the table version of foosball. This stipulation also includes the two goalies. The activity should be conducted in the shallow section of the pool. Each participant should only be in chest-high water.

Preparation: The activity requires a beach ball, two whistles, and two goals.

Number of Participants: Two teams of nine people per team

Age Range and Swimming Level of Participants: Ages 12 and older who have strong swimming skills

Safety Precautions: Two adult activity leaders should referee the game to encourage safety and good sportsmanship. All participants, spectators, and referees should follow the commands and directions of the supervising lifeguard(s).

Game #53: One-on-One Water Soccer

Objective: To develop eye-hand coordination, ball control, and sportsmanship

Goals of Participants: To move a soccer ball on the water past an opponent and into the goal

Overview: Two participants play against each other, trying to get the ball into the other participant's goal. Because the activity only uses one goal to score in, the participants play half-court. After a participant makes a goal, his opponent takes the soccer ball to the top of the court to begin play. The ball has to stay on the water surface until the offensive player nears the goal, at which point it can then be thrown into the goal. The defensive player can use his hands to either try to block the soccer ball or catch it. A point is awarded for each goal scored. The game is played until one participant earns 12 points.

Rules: The defensive participant cannot come in contact with the player with the ball. Possession of the ball can only be transferred, if the defending player can take the ball without touching the offensive player.

Preparation: The activity requires a soccer ball and a plastic goal.

Number of Participants: Two players

Age Range and Swimming Level of Participants: Ages 12 and older who have strong swimming skills

Safety Precautions: Both players should use caution when they play near the soccer goal in order to not come too close to the wall of the pool.

Game #54: Water Golf

Objective: To teach creativity by practicing golf skills in an adapted golfing environment

Goals of Participants: To land a plastic practice golf ball on a homemade golf green that is floating in the center of the swimming pool

Overview: Each golfer stands on the pool deck and softly hits a plastic ball, using a putter, onto a floating green. The floating green is a three-foot-by-three-foot section of thick plywood, with a small hoop lying on the center of the wood surface.

Rules: To score a point, each golfer must get his ball inside the hoop. The participant with the most points wins the game. Five points is the highest score available. In the case of a tie, the players who have tied participate in another round of the game to break the tie.

Preparation: Each golfer gets five balls to hit into the hoop. A piece of carpet or rug should be placed on the pool deck that players hit from in order to prevent damaging the pool deck with the putter.

Number of Participants: Up to 25 players

Age Range and Swimming Level of Participants: Ages 12 and older; non-swimmers can participate in the activity.

Safety Precautions: Water golf should only be played when no other individuals are in the pool. Spectators should stand 20 feet away from the golfer. Everyone in the pool area should follow the commands and directions of the supervising lifeguard(s).

6

Teambuilding Water Games

Game #55: Save the Whale

Objective: To work as a team to retrieve an object within a set boundary

Goals of Participants: To find a way to reach a toy whale that is floating in the center of a roped-off area

Overview: The activity involves roping off an eight-foot section with polypropylene rope that floats on the surface of the water. The basic goal of the game is to have participants save the toy whale that is floating in the center of the roped-off area, without any member of the team going inside or underneath the roped-off section.

Rules: Team members cannot use the lifesaving equipment from the swimming pool for this activity. Participants cannot dive under the rope to retrieve the whale. The rope boundaries cannot be physically moved or altered by the team. One viable option for solving this challenge would be to create an undercurrent or waves that would propel the toy whale to exit the roped-off area. On the other hand, participants should determine an appropriate method for addressing the problem on their own.

Preparation: The activity requires a floatable toy whale and eight feet of polypropylene rope that is tied in a loop.

Number of Participants: A team up to 10 people

Age Range and Swimming Level of Participants: Ages 12 and older who have strong swimming skills

Safety Precautions: Adult activity leaders should be in the water to help ensure that participants do not get tangled in the rope or that the rope becomes a hazard. No other individuals should be in the pool while the game is being conducted.

Game #56: Underwater Hoop Pass

Objective: To join forces with team members to accomplish a task as quickly as possible and then subsequently improve that performance during other attempts

Goals of Participants: To pass a hoop around a circle of team members

Overview: A group of 10 people, holding hands in the shallow-end of the swimming pool, form a circle. A hoop is passed from one person to another within the circle of hands. The interlinking chain of hand grasps cannot be broken as the hoop is passed. Standing in chest-high water, each participant has to step through the hoop as it is passed around the group.

Rules: The first round of the game is for practice and is performed at a relatively slow pace, as team members communicate with each other to give instructions concerning how to step through the hoop in chest-high water. The second round is a timed event that involves determining how long it takes the team to move the hoop within the circle of team members. The third round of the game focuses on improving the team's performance and lowering the time achieved in the second round. As such, the team is competing against its own previous times. Both the second and third rounds of the game are timed.

Preparation: The activity requires a large hoop and a stopwatch.

Number of Participants: A team up to 10 people

Age Range and Swimming Level of Participants: Ages 12 and older who have strong swimming skills

Safety Precautions: No team member should feel forced to complete this task. A decision to watch, instead of participate, should be respected.

Game #57: Torpedo

Objective: To listen and trust other team members who are giving directions and instructions

Goals of Participants: To help other team members navigate, while blindfolded, through a maze of floating foam-noodle torpedoes

Overview: In the shallow-end of the swimming pool, the team is divided in half. Half of a team's members are positioned on one side of the swimming pool, while the remaining members are located on the opposite side. Both groups line up facing each other, with their backs against the pool wall. Each participant looks across the pool at the person who is directly across from him, who is designated as his partner. In between the two groups, 25 foam noodles that no one is allowed to touch are floating in the pool. Adult activity leaders determine which side starts first in walking through the sea of floating noodles, while blindfolded and being coached by their partners on the other side.

Rules: If a blindfolded participant touches a floating foam noodle (torpedo), he must return to the starting area and resume walking through the course again. The individual who is giving instructional directions has to remain stationary until the first round of the game is over. On the second round of the game, the two partners switch roles—the former blindfolded participant then guides his former coach through the course.

Preparation: The activity requires five blindfolds and 25 foam noodles.

Number of Participants: A team up to 10 people

Age Range and Swimming Level of Participants: Ages 12 and older who have strong swimming skills

Safety Precautions: If, at any point of the game, a blindfolded participant becomes distressed or disoriented, he can remove his blindfold and discontinue his involvement in the activity.

Game #58: Aqua Ball

Objective: To promote team unity and symmetric (give and take) communication

Goals of Participants: To work with teammates to devise a way to transport an exercise ball from one side of the pool and back without anyone using his hands

Overview: The group's participants divide in half to form two lines in rows that face each other in the shallow section of the swimming pool. The person across the row from each participant serves as the participant's partner. Each two-person partnership holds a beach towel that they use to transport the large ball to the next twosome. The process continues until the ball is moved to the opposite side of the pool and then back to the starting area.

Rules: Only the beach towels can touch the exercise ball. If the ball touches one of the team members, the ball then goes back to the starting point, and the team begins again.

Preparation: The activity requires five beach towels and an exercise ball.

Number of Participants: A team up to 10 people

Age Range and Swimming Level of Participants: Ages 12 and older who have strong swimming skills

Safety Precautions: Participants on the end of the line should use caution as the ball approaches them, so that they do not become trapped between the ball and the pool wall.

Game #59: Flotsam and Jetsam

Objective: To mobilize the team as quickly as possible in cleaning up the debris (colored balls) in a quick and efficient manner from the swimming pool

Goals of Participants: To gather colored balls into groups and deposit them in color-coded buckets

Overview: Prior to the activity beginning, 50 plastic baseball-size balls of assorted colors (e.g., red, blue, yellow, and green) are dumped into the pool. The team is timed, while attempting to retrieve the floating balls and put them into corresponding color-coded buckets that are positioned on the deck of the swimming pool.

Rules: Once the team has initially accomplished its task, participants perform the same task again, trying to decrease the amount of time it takes to complete the assigned task. Between rounds, the team has five minutes to strategize on how to best accomplish the task. The second chance for a team to improve its efforts should incorporate enhanced efforts involving leadership, delegation, and communication.

Preparation: The activity requires 50 balls of assorted colors (e.g., red, blue, yellow, green, etc.), as well as four buckets that correspond to the colors of the balls used in the game.

Number of Participants: A team up to 10 people

Age Range and Swimming Level of Participants: Ages 12 and older who have strong swimming skills

Safety Precautions: An activity leader should be in the pool to retrieve balls that float to the deep-end.

Game #60: Bridge

Objective: To provide an opportunity to problem-solve by getting ideas from all team members

Goals of Participants: To get an exercise ball from one side of the swimming pool to the other side without it touching the water

Overview: Using two 25-foot sections of rope, team members straddle a ball in the middle of the two rope sections and transport it from one side of the pool to the other side. Team members are positioned on both sides of the pool on the deck. Their basic task involves maneuvering the rope back and forth to allow the ball to move in between the rope lines. If the gap between the lines is too big, the ball will fall in the water, and the team will have to start over again.

Rules: The ball cannot be thrown from one side of the pool to the other. It has to roll on top of the rope the entire time. In addition, the team cannot lob the ball to the other side by using the rope.

Preparation: The activity requires a large exercise ball and two 25-foot sections of rope, such as dynamic climbing rope.

Number of Participants: A team up to 10 people

Age Range and Swimming Level of Participants: Ages 12 and older; non-swimmers can participate in the activity if they wear life jackets.

Safety Precautions: Participants on the opposite side of the swimming pool should not attempt to pull other team members into the water by tugging on the rope. The game should be stopped if this type of behavior occurs.

Game #61: Mariner's Pride

Objective: To plan, design, and build an object that is functional and durable

Goals of Participants: To involve all team members in the effort to make a miniature raft that floats

Overview: The team builds a raft, using 20 craft sticks and two feet of artificial sinew that is used to lash the sticks together. The raft must be large enough to hold a nine-ounce empty paper cup. The raft must hold the cup in an upright position as it floats in the water.

Rules: The team has 10 minutes to build a seaworthy raft that will be used in the game (i.e., #62: Land Ahoy).

Preparation: The activity requires 20 craft sticks, two feet of artificial sinew, a nine-ounce paper cup, and scissors.

Number of Participants: A team up to 10 people

Age Range and Swimming Level of Participants: Ages eight and older; non-swimmers can participate in the activity.

Safety Precautions: Any child under the age of 12 who is a non-swimmer must wear a life jacket.

Game #62: Land Ahoy

Objective: To value other people's viewpoint and perspective

Goals of Participants: To float the raft that was made in the previous game (#61: Mariner's Pride), while looking through the wrong end of a pair of binoculars

Overview: Each team member guides the raft by creating small waves, using one hand near the raft. A pair of binoculars is in the other hand. The participant looks through the wrong end of the binoculars in order to create a scenario in which the raft looks very small and the distance to the opposite side of the pool (i.e., the shore) seems far away. When the participant reaches the other side of the pool, he hands the binoculars and the raft to the next team member to float the raft back to the other side. The process continues until everyone on the team has performed the assigned task. At the end of the game, adult leaders can discuss how this activity is somewhat like trying to understand someone else's point of view that is different than their own. Furthermore, with time and patience, gaining an enhanced level of understanding—just like reaching the other side of the pool—can be achieved.

Rules: Team members should walk very slowly while performing the game, since their visual balance has been altered by the change in perspective that results from looking through the wrong end of the binoculars.

Preparation: The activity requires a miniature raft or boat and a pair of binoculars.

Number of Participants: A team up to 10 people

Age Range and Swimming Level of Participants: Ages eight and older; non-swimmers must wear a life jacket.

Safety Precautions: If at any point of the game a participant becomes distressed or disoriented, he can stop looking through the binoculars and discontinue being engaged in the activity.

Game #63: Team Water Craft

Objective: To use creativity and imagination while racing collectively as a team in achieving the overall best time for the team

Goals of Participants: To perform the race as different types of human water crafts. At the end of the race all team members join in to make a human ship.

Overview: The game begins with one team member, pretending to be a jet ski, running or swimming in the shallow-end of the swimming pool toward an orange cone positioned on the deck at the opposite side of the pool and back to the starting area. At this point, he tags another team member. The two of them then run in single file, like they are in a canoe. Together, they race to the orange cone and return back to the starting area. They pretend to paddle the whole way. When the two participants return, they tag the third participant. This time, the team races in a reverse-pyramid formation that represents a boat with two passengers riding in front of the boat and a water skier trailing behind. The threesome then runs to the orange cone and back, before tagging the fourth, and final, participant. The entire four-person team makes a human ship with one person at the bow of the ship (the front person), two participants in the middle, and one person in the back (i.e., the stern of the ship). Two people are in the middle; the individual on the right side is the starboard side of the ship, while the person on the left is the port side. The two team members who are the bow and the stern of the ship put their hands together to form a point, so that the group takes on a ship formation. At this point, the entire team "sails" to the orange cone and back to the starting area. The event is timed. The team then performs the task again in an attempt to improve their time from their first effort.

Rules: Team members only race alongside or near each other. They do not try to hold hands as they race together.

Preparation: The activity requires a stopwatch and an orange cone.

Number of Participants: A team of four people

Age Range and Swimming Level of Participants: Ages 12 and older who have strong swimming skills

Safety Precautions: Participants should race only as fast as the slowest person, in order to keep from colliding with fellow team members.

Game #64: The Not-So-Deserted Island

Objective: To join forces as a team to accomplish a specific task for a certain time period

Goals of Participants: To perform an assigned task, while standing on a cookie sheet with teammates

Overview: Positioned in the shallow-end of the swimming pool, team members hold hands with each other, as the entire team tries collectively to stand together on a flat cookie sheet. The cookie sheet represents a "not-so-deserted island."

Rules: Once the entire team is on the "island," participants have to sing Row, Row, Row Your Boat three times before anyone is allowed to leave the "island."

Preparation: The activity requires a flat cookie sheet, with no edges.

Number of Participants: Four to eight participants

Age Range and Swimming Level of Participants: Ages 12 and older who have strong swimming skills

Safety Precautions: Each team member should have his head and shoulders above the water at all times during the game. Everyone's feet should be touching the cookie sheet. Anyone who is uncomfortable during this game should be allowed to cheer the team on as a spectator.

Game #65: Giant Ring Toss

Objective: To teach accountability concerning the role that each individual has on the team's overall success or failure

Goals of Participants: To throw hoops at assigned cones

Overview: Each team member is assigned a hoop of a specific color and a matching cone. When it is his turn in the game, the participant must throw his hoop onto the corresponding colored cone that is positioned on the pool deck. The participant must continue throwing the hoop until it lands on the cone. The next person in line cannot throw his hoop, until the previous individual has completed the assigned task. One team member is positioned on the pool deck to retrieve any hoops that have missed the cone and return them to the participant who is currently throwing.

Rules: Team members should encourage and cheer on their teammates. Each participant should stand three feet away from the edge of the swimming pool when throwing. All of the hoops should be the same size. The event is timed to see how long it takes for each member of the team to complete the task. When the game is over, the team is given a second chance to perform the task, in an attempt to improve its time.

Preparation: The activity requires a different colored hoop, a matching cone for each member of the team, and one stopwatch.

Number of Participants: A team up to 10 people

Age Range and Swimming Level of Participants: Ages eight and older; non-swimmers can participate in the activity.

Safety Precautions: Participants and spectators should be cautioned to stay alert during the entire activity in order to keep from getting hit by a flying hoop.

Game #66: Colossal Ball

Objective: To learn to be attentive and focused, while performing a task with others

Goals of Participants: To work as a team to keep a large ball in the air

Overview: Using a large seven-foot inflatable ball, team members keep the ball in the air for five consecutive minutes, while standing in the pool. The activity is times. If the ball touches the water or lands on the pool deck, the time restarts.

Rules: Team members cannot hold the ball longer than three seconds. They should hold the ball just long enough to push it back in the air.

Preparation: The activity requires one seven-foot inflatable ball, an air pump, and a stopwatch.

Number of Participants: A team up to 10 people

Age Range and Swimming Level of Participants: Ages 12 and older who have strong swimming skills

Safety Precautions: Participants should avoid standing near the pool walls in order to keep from being trapped and possibly injured between the walls and the ball. No other individuals should be in the pool, while the game is being conducted.

Game #67: Loch Ness Monster

Objective: To design a floating object, using the collective input of team members

Goals of Participants: To make a small replica of the Loch Ness monster

Overview: The team is positioned in the shallow-end of the pool and is given basic office supplies to make a model of the Loch Ness monster. The team has a five-minute planning session to divide up assignments and an additional 10 minutes to construct the monster.

Rules: The monster should be able to float on its own. The team makes waves for the montster to reach the opposite side of the swimming pool.

Preparation: The activity requires three large and six small Styrofoam balls, 10 toothpicks, 100 large rubber bands, and 10 pipe cleaners of assorted colors.

Number of Participants: A team up to 10 people

Age Range and Swimming Level of Participants: Ages six and older; non-swimmers can participate in the activity.

Safety Precautions: Team members should use caution to keep from spilling any building materials that might cause a possible injury to the participants or damage to the pool's filtration system.

Game #68: Boat Rescue

Objective: To learn to cooperate, while simultaneously working together to solve a problem

Goals of Participants: To scoop a toy boat out of the water, using a lacrosse stick

Overview: A small boat is positioned in the water, about two feet from the pool wall. All participants are standing on the pool deck, holding onto the same lacrosse stick. In a collective effort, everyone on the team must hold onto the stick and work together to try to retrieve the boat from the pool. When the boat is lifted out of the water, it should be gently laid on the deck of the pool.

Rules: If the boat drifts away from the lacrosse stick, the team should attempt to bring it back by paddling the lacrosse stick toward the participants in order draw the boat into an undercurrent toward the deck. An adult leader may be positioned in the pool to assist the group if the boat drifts too far away and must be brought back closer to the team.

Preparation: The activity requires a toy boat and a lacrosse stick.

Number of Participants: A team up to four people. Multiple teams can perform the game simultaneously in different areas of the swimming pool.

Age Range and Swimming Level of Participants: Ages six and older; non-swimmers can participate in the activity if they wear life jackets.

Safety Precautions: All team members should be alert during the activity to keep from losing their balance and falling in the pool or avoid being injured with the lacrosse stick.

Game: #69: Sailor's Crossing

Objective: To learn to work quickly and carefully as fragile items are transported from one team member to another

Goals of Participants: To carry a paper cup, brimming full of small ice cubes

Overview: Half of the team is positioned on one side of the shallow-end of the swimming pool, and the other half is on the opposite side. Each participant walks from one side of the pool to the opposite side, carrying a cup of ice cubes. Once the first participant reaches the opposite side of the pool, he hands the cup to another team member, who then walks to the opposite side. The process continues until every team member has carried the cup.

Rules: The ice cubes are counted before the event and then re-counted after the activity to determine if the team had lost any of the ice, while transporting the cup from one team member to another.

Preparation: The activity requires one nine-ounce paper cup, filled with pebbled ice cubes.

Number of Participants: A team up to four people

Age Range and Swimming Level of Participants: Ages eight and older; non-swimmers can participate in the activity.

Safety Precautions: The ice cubes should only be carried in the cup. They should not be held in a participant's hand or mouth. Participants should not eat the ice.

Game #70: H$_2$0 Cargo

Objective: To learn to communicate and cooperate, while attempting to transport an unstable item

Goals of Participants: To carry an item on a platform that has rope handles

Overview: Positioned in the shallow-end of the swimming pool, team members transport a plastic water bottle on a one-foot wooden platform that has rope handles. During the activity, each member of the team holds onto a rope handle. The entire team attempts to walk collectively from one side of the pool to the other side without the plastic bottle tipping over.

Rules: The rope handles are three-feet long. Team members must stand three feet from the wooden platform at all times. If the cargo (the water bottle) tips over into the pool, the team has to return to the starting point and restart the game.

Preparation: The activity requires seven rope handles, made from polypropylene rope, that are attached to a one-foot circular wooden platform; the activity also requires a plastic water bottle full of water.

Number of Participants: A team of seven people

Age Range and Swimming Level of Participants: Ages 12 and older; non-swimmers can participate in the activity.

Safety Precautions: The activity should be conducted in chest-high water. No other individuals should be in the pool while the game is being played in order to keep them from getting tangled in the rope handles.

7

Tag Games

Game #71: Iceberg Tag

Objective: To create a light-hearted environment in which participants play and exhibit good sportsmanship

Goals of Participants: To avoid being tagged by the person who is designated as "it"

Overview: The participant who is "it" chases all of the other participants in the shallow-end of the swimming pool. If the person who is "it" touches someone on the shoulder, that person is then "frozen" like an iceberg and has to stand stationary, with his legs far apart. The frozen person can be rescued by another participant, who swims underwater and between the frozen person's legs. The frozen person is then no longer stationary and can resume playing the game.

Rules: The game is over when the person who is "it" tags everyone in the group or the game has lasted 10 minutes. After 10 minutes, the activity leader selects a new person to be "it." The last person tagged in the game is the individual who is "it" for the start of the next round.

Preparation: Prior to the game, one person is selected to be "it." One way to determine who will serve as the first "it" is to have the participants form a circle, with an adult leader in the middle of the circle. The leader says, "Ice cubes, ice cubes in a dish, how many pieces do you wish?" The leader then points at one person in the circle to give a reply to the question. If this person replies "five," for example, the leader then points clockwise and counts, "one, two, three, four, five, and you are now it." The last person to whom the leader is pointing is designated as the first person to be "it" for the first round of tag.

Number of Participants: A group up to 15 people

Age Range and Swimming Level of Participants: Ages eight and older who have strong swimming skills

Safety Precautions: Participants should be cautioned to use care and sound judgment when swimming underwater. The person who is "it" cannot tag a participant while the participant is underwater.

Game #72: Marine Life Tag

Objective: To learn the names of different fish, animals, birds, and other marine life that live in or near the ocean

Goals of Participants: To avoid being tagged by the person who is designated as "it"

Overview: The participant who is "it" chases and tries to tag all of the other participants, who run from him in the shallow-end of the swimming pool. As the person who is "it" approaches a participant in an attempt to tag him on the shoulder, this person can avoid being tagged if he can yell out a name of a fish, bird, or animal before getting tagged. Individuals who can do this cannot be tagged. Those who can't do this can be tagged, which precludes them from playing anymore the rest of the game. The first person tagged in the game is the person who is "it" for the next round of the game.

Rules: The game is over either when the person who is "it" has tagged everyone in the group or the game has lasted 10 minutes. After 10 minutes, the activity leader selects a new person to be "it."

Preparation: Prior to the game, one person is selected to be "it." One way to determine who will serve as the first "it" is to have the adult leader hold the same number of plastic straws in his hand as there are people playing the game. Participants can only see the top of the straws that are being held in the adult leader's hand. One of the straws is half as long as all of the rest of the straws. One at a time, participants choose a straw. The individual who selects the short straw is the person who is designated as "it" for the first round of the game.

Number of Participants: A group up to 15 people

Age Range and Swimming Level of Participants: Ages eight and older

Safety Precautions: The person who is "it" cannot push or shove while attempting to tag participants.

Game #73: One, Two, Three . . . Mermaid

Objective: To reinforce the need for being alert and prepared when responding quickly, while performing a task

Goals of Participants: To avoid being caught by the person who is designated as "it"

Overview: A group of participants stand in a circle in the shallow-end of the swimming pool. The person who is "it" stands behind the group and pats each person on the back of the head, while counting "one, two, three" . . .—up to as high as he wants until he says the word "mermaid." The individual who had his head patted while the word mermaid was said by the person who is "it" then leaves his spot and is chased around the circle by the person who is "it," until he is either caught or returns to his original spot.

Rules: The person who has been tagged by the person who is "it" is now the new "it" for the next round of the game.

Preparation: Prior to the activity, one person is selected to be "it." One way to determine who will serve as the first "it" is to ask each participant before the game to think of a number from one to 10. The individual who is closest to a number predetermined by an adult leader is the person who is "it" for the first round of the game.

Number of Participants: A group of up to 10 people

Age Range and Swimming Level of Participants: Ages eight and older who have strong swimming skills

Safety Precautions: Participants should be spaced out far enough in the circle so that plenty of room exists for the participant who is running in an attempt to return to his original spot, without colliding with others.

Game #74: Sitting Duck

Objective: To develop eye-hand coordination, catching, and passing skills

Goals of Participants: To keep an object away from the person who is "it"

Overview: One person is "it" in a group of three participants. The other two participants stand on either side of the person who is "it," trying to keep a large rubber duck from being caught from the person who is "it" by throwing the duck over his head.

Rules: If the person who is "it" catches the duck, then the last person to throw the duck is the new "it" for the next round of the game. The positions of the participants should be rotated if the original person who is "it" is still in the middle after 10 minutes.

Preparation: Prior to the game, one person is selected to be "it." One way to determine who will serve as the first "it" is to have the three participants in the activity attempt to say as fast as possible "Not it." The last individual to do so is the participant who is "it." The activity requires a large rubber duck.

Number of Participants: Three participants

Age Range and Swimming Level of Participants: Ages eight and older who have strong swimming skills

Safety Precautions: Adult leaders should monitor the game closely in order to prevent teasing or taunting by the two players against the person who is "it."

Game #75: Fishing Net Tag

Objective: To emphasize the value of listening skills as a set of instructions are given at the beginning of the game

Goals of Participants: To avoid being tagged by the person who is "it" or his imaginary fishing net

Overview: The person who is "it" is the fisherman. Everyone else is a fish, trying not to get caught in the fisherman's net. The net is an invisible barrier that is always directly in front of the fisherman wherever he is facing. This barrier is the width of the fisherman's body and extends from where the fisherman is currently standing to the nearest pool wall directly opposite to the fisherman.

Rules: Participants who are fish cannot cross or be standing in front of the fisherman. Otherwise, they will be automatically tagged and have to stand stationary where they were caught for the entire game. The fisherman can move around and tag any participant on the shoulder, who will then have to stand stationary for the game. The first participant to be tagged by the fisherman's net is the individual who is "it" for the next round of the game. Participants trying to avoid the net will still be tagged if they go underwater, but are still in front of the fisherman. The fisherman cannot go in circles trying to tag everyone in the pool with one continuous loop. He has to stand still and count to the number five every time he changes positions. Participants who do not listen and adhere to instructions for the game quickly learn the consequences of their actions, since they become tagged easier and earlier than those individuals who listen and prepare for the game properly.

Preparation: Prior to the game, one person is selected to be "it." One way to determine who will serve as the first "it" is to have an adult leader require each participant to roll a pair of dice on the pool deck. Whoever gets the highest number is the person who is "it." If participants tie for the highest number, they continue rolling the dice until one individual earns the "it" designation.

Number of Participants: Up to 15 people

Age Range and Swimming Level of Participants: Ages eight and older who have strong swimming skills

Safety Precautions: The boundaries of the game should be limited to only the shallow-end of the swimming pool.

Game #76: Swimming Cap Tag

Objective: To learn to carefully search for someone, with the emphasis on accuracy, rather than speed

Goals of Participants: To find an individual within the number of attempts allowed

Overview: In a corner of the shallow-end of the swimming pool, the participants play in a small area. Each of the individuals crouch down so that only his head is above water. Wearing a swimming cap on his head, one person serves as "home base." This person can see, but cannot talk during the game. The person who is "home base" also has to stand stationary during the activity. All of the other participants move around in the tight area, with their eyes closed. They also are not allowed to talk. These participants are trying to find the "home base" (the individual with the swimming cap on) by gently touching the heads of other players. Once they find "home base," they open their eyes and swim to the opposite side of the pool to watch until the game is over. Each participant is given three practice tries to find "home base." On his fourth try, if he still does not find the player wearing a swimming cap ("home base"), he is out of the game.

Rules: When a participant is out of the game, he opens his eyes, swims to the opposite side of the pool, and watches the game from a distance. When participants are out of the game or have already found "home base," they cannot talk and give any instructions to the participants who are still playing.

Preparation: All participants, including the person who is "home base," wear swimming goggles for eye protection. The individual who is "home base" also wears a swimming cap.

Number of Participants: Up to 10 players

Age Range and Swimming Level of Participants: Ages eight and older who have strong swimming skills

Safety Precautions: To avoid possible injuries, participants should move around relatively slowly, while searching for the person wearing the swimming cap. Each participant should walk with his hands to his side until he bumps into someone. Even then, he should be careful when reaching for that individual's head in order to avoid poking the person in the face. Five adult leaders should form a human fence in the swimming pool to establish boundaries to help participants stay in the shallow-end of the pool.

Game #77: Steal the Buoy

Objective: To teach sportsmanship and build team spirit

Goals of Participants: To take a floating ball from the center of the pool before another team can retrieve it

Overview: Prior to the game, the participants are divided into two teams of equal size. Each team member gets a number assigned to him, starting with number one and continuing up to number 10. Each team has a member with the same number. For example, two people have number one, two people have number two, etc. The ball serves as the "buoy" and is placed in the center of the shallow-end of the swimming pool. Both teams line up against the swimming pool wall on opposite sides of the pool. To start the game, an adult leader yells out a number, which is a signal for the two members on both teams with that number to race toward the ball to attempt to "steal" it first.

Rules: The first person to take the ball races back to his team. The other person who did not grab the ball then has to pause and count to five before chasing after the first person. If the person with the ball reaches his team before being tagged, his team receives a point. If the person who is chasing the person with the ball tags him before he reaches his team, his team receives a point. The game is played until one of the teams reaches 10 points.

Preparation: The activity requires one large playground ball

Number of Participants: Two teams of 10 people per team

Age Range and Swimming Level of Participants: Ages eight and older who have strong swimming skills

Safety Precautions: Players should be cautioned to avoid running into the pool wall as they race back to their team if they retrieve the "buoy." Individuals who are chasing an opponent should be warned not to push or shove as they are trying to tag the person.

Game #78: Blind Man's Bluff

Objective: To find someone within a swimming pool setting while blindfolded

Goals of Participants: To escape from the person who is "it"

Overview: With his eyes closed, the person who is "it" tries to find the rest of the participants who are scattered around the shallow-end of the swimming pool.

Rules: All participants must stand within six to 10 feet of the person who is "it" at all times. Only the person who is "it" is allowed to talk. Each individual who is touched on the arm by the person who is "it" is out of the game and quietly gets out of the pool and waits for a new round of the game, while sitting on the pool deck. The first person tagged is the "it" for the next round of the game.

Preparation: Prior to the game, one person is selected to be "it." One way to determine who will serve as the first "it" is to determine which participant's birthday is closest to the current date and designate that person as "it" for the first game.

Number of Participants: A group up to 10 people

Age Range and Swimming Level of Participants: Ages eight and older who have strong swimming skills

Safety Precautions: Five leaders should form a human fence in the swimming pool to establish boundaries to help the person who is "it" stay in the shallow-end of the pool.

Game #79: Noah's Ark Tag

Objective: To develop keen listen skills, in an environment with excessive noise and distraction

Goals of Participants: To find the person with the same animal assignment

Overview: The participants are divided into two smaller teams of equal size. Each team has its own leader. The two teams face each other on opposite ends of the shallow-end of the swimming pool. Each participant is given an animal assignment that he needs to imitate the sound of. Each team has a cow, tiger, duck, pig, frog, lion, rooster, monkey, bear, and dog. Once the assignments have been made, each participant closes his eyes and has to make the sound of his animal in order to find the person on the opposite team who has the same animal sound as he has.

Rules: Participants slowly walk towards the animal sounds made by their counterpart. Once they tag each other they can open their eyes and wait for the other group members to tag their partners.

Preparation: The activity requires a list of animals.

Number of Participants: A group up to 20 people

Age Range and Swimming Level of Participants: Ages eight and older who have strong swimming skills

Safety Precautions: Five adult leaders should form a human fence in the swimming pool to establish boundaries to help the participants stay in the shallow-end of the pool.

Game #80: Echo Tag

Objective: To develop listening skills for non-verbal communication

Goals of Participants: To not get tagged by the person who is "it"

Overview: In the shallow-end of the swimming pool, the person who is "it" tries to tag all of the other participants with his eyes closed. No one can talk in the game. The way that the "it" attempts to find where people are at is to clap twice, which causes the rest of the group to respond by clapping twice back. Once the person who is "it" hears his "echo," he tries to tag the person who is closest to him.

Rules: When a participant is tagged, he is out of the game. The first person to be tagged is the "it" for the next round.

Preparation: Prior to the game, one person is selected to be the "it." One way to determine who will serve as the first "it" is to have an adult leader have a cloth bag of marbles, all blue, except for one green marble. The bag has the same number of marbles as there are participants in the game. Each participant must grab a marble out of the bag. The participant who pulls the green marble out of the bag is designated as the "it" for the first round of the game.

Number of Participants: A group up to 10 people

Age Range and Swimming Level of Participants: Ages eight and older who have strong swimming skills

Safety Precautions: Five adult leaders should form a human fence in the swimming pool to establish boundaries to help the person who is "it" stay in the shallow-end of the pool.

8

Nautical Games

Game #81: Sea Legs

Objective: To provide an "ice breaker" game

Goals of Participants: To match the feet with a person hiding behind a curtain

Overview: The activity is held on the pool deck as an "ice breaker" game to create a playful environment for other events that will be held in the swimming pool. On the deck, two leaders hold up a bed sheet to create a curtain. The participants are divided into two smaller teams of equal size. All of the players on the first team are positioned behind the curtain, with one person standing near the curtain, with his feet exposed, so that the other team can attempt to guess who he is.

Rules: The team that is guessing is given three opportunities to guess who belongs to the pair of feet. A team gets one point if its members guess correctly. The team behind the curtain gets a point anytime its opponents cannot identify whose feet they are. The first team to reach 20 points wins the game.

Preparation: The activity requires a flat queen sheet.

Number of Participants: Two teams of 15 people per team

Age Range and Swimming Level of Participants: Ages six and older; non-swimmers can participate in the activity.

Safety Precautions: The activity should be conducted several yards away from the swimming pool so it doesn't interfere with the pool operations.

Game #82: Water Balloon Catch

Objective: To develop partnerships that work together to help their team to win the game

Goals of Participants: To toss a water balloon over a net to the opposing team

Overview: A pennant string is set up three feet over the pool to serve as a net. The participants are divided into two teams of equal size. Each team tosses a water balloon over the net to the opposing team. Members of each team are grouped into partnerships who share a beach towel with which they catch water balloons and which they use to lob the water balloons back over the net.

Rules: If a water balloon pops on the side of a team, the other team earns a point. The first team to reach 10 points wins the game.

Preparation: The activity requires pennant string and 50 small water balloons.

Number of Participants: Two teams of equal size, with up to 10 people per team

Age Range and Swimming Level of Participants: Ages 12 and older who have strong swimming skills

Safety Precautions: Participants should be cautioned to be alert during the game to prevent them from getting hit by an incoming water balloon. Participants also should immediately discard any broken pieces of balloon into a trash can to prevent them from getting into the pool's filtration system. The game should be the only activity in the swimming pool at the time. All participants should follow the commands and directions of the lifeguard(s).

Game #83: King Neptune's Sea

Objective: To provide an opportunity to strategize in an attempt to outguess an opponent

Goals of Participants: To be at the right place and the right time to avoid being eliminated from the game for as long as possible

Overview: One person is designated as King Neptune, ruler of the sea, who gets angry when he finds trespassers in his waters. King Neptune closes his eyes and counts to 20, causing the other participants to scrabble into four designated areas of the pool. With his eyes still closed, King Neptune points to one of the designated areas. He then opens his eyes and whoever is in that section is out of the game. When King Neptune closes his eyes again, participants identify another section to be in, but this time, they can only choose three of the sections. Once again, King Neptune points and eliminates a section of the pool and the people who are in it. The third round is the last round of the game. At this point, participants have two choices. If no one is in the section that King Neptune points at, King Neptune remains "it" for another round. On the other hand, if he catches someone in a section, he can choose whom his replacement will be for the next round of the game.

Rules: Participants can only move when King Neptune has his eyes closed. Once King Neptune opens his eyes, all players must stay in their current section. Participants who have been eliminated from their section must leave the pool and watch the rest of the game from the pool deck.

Preparation: Prior to the start of the game, the four sections of the swimming pool for the activity must be designated.

Number of Participants: Up to 20 people

Age Range and Swimming Level of Participants: Ages eight and older who have strong swimming skills

Safety Precautions: Participants should not push or shove each other as they go from one section to another.

Game #84: Haunted Bayou

Objective: To create a spooky, but safe, atmosphere for a nighttime pool activity

Goals of Participants: To not get caught by the ghost of the bayou

Overview: Prior to the game, one participant is selected to be the ghost of the bayou, although no one knows who he is. He is among the group, as they walk around the pool singing "There is no ghost out tonight; Daddy scared him away last night." Then, when everyone least expects it, the ghost yells "Boo" and starts to chase participants, trying to catch them. Participants can go to "home base"—the main swimming pool steps—to avoid getting caught by the ghost.

Rules: Anyone caught by the ghost is out of the game. The first person caught serves as the ghost for the next round of the game.

Preparation: Prior to the game, green, blue, red, and yellow glow sticks are set inside of several plastic Jack O' Lanterns, which are then placed on the pool deck to make the game extra creepy looking.

Number of Participants: Up to 20 people

Age Range and Swimming Level of Participants: Ages eight and older who have strong swimming skills

Safety Precautions: The swimming pool lights must remain on during the activity, so that the lifeguards can scan the area, including the bottom of the pool.

Game #85: London Bridge Is Falling Down

Objective: To provide an opportunity for younger children to increase their comfort level swimming underwater

Goals of Participants: To swim a short distance underwater

Overview: The game is played in the shallow-end of the swimming pool, where two adult leaders face each other and form an arm bridge that is extended up to allow children to pass under their arms. During the activity, the nursery rhyme is sung by the group. Subsequently, the arm bridge is lowered down to the water's surface on the last word of the rhyme, in an attempt to capture one child who has to swim underwater under the arm bridge to escape.

Rules: The adult leaders should choose a different person each time to capture in their arm bridge.

Preparation: Prior to the game, the adult leaders should review the lyrics of the nursery rhyme.

Number of Participants: Up to 20 people

Age Range and Swimming Level of Participants: Ages six and older who have beginning swimming skills

Safety Precautions: The adult leaders should be sensitive to each child's skill level and/or level of fear regarding swimming underwater and take that into consideration when selecting participants for the activity.

Game #86: Lighthouse

Objective: To play a hide-and-seek type activity at night, in which participants use skill and strategy to stay in the game

Goals of Participants: To avoid getting caught by the individual designated as the "lighthouse"

Overview: The game is played at night. One person serves as the "lighthouse." Holding a flashlight and standing stationary on the pool deck five feet from the pool, he tries to indentify swimmers by shining a flashlight at them.

Rules: If the "lighthouse" properly identifies a participant, that individual is out of the game. The first person who is caught by the "lighthouse" assumes that position for the next round of the game. Participants can hide underwater only three times, for a maximum of five seconds each time. The rest of the time, each participant must swim around, with all of his head out of water.

Preparation: The activity requires a flashlight for the person who is the "lighthouse."

Number of Participants: Up to 30 people

Age Range and Swimming Level of Participants: Ages eight and older who have strong swimming skills

Safety Precautions: The swimming pool lights should remain on during the activity, so that lifeguards can scan the area, including the bottom of the pool. The flashlight should not be allowed to interfere with the lifeguard's ability to see clearly.

Game #87: Water Spots

Objective: To create a fun and whimsical environment, one in which everyone is constantly changing his location throughout the game

Goals of Participants: To find a water spot to stand on in order to stay in the game

Overview: Prior to the game, activity leaders place vinyl spots in the shallow-end of the pool on the floor in the form of a circle, with one less spot than the number of participants. One person, designated as the "it," doesn't have a water spot; he stands in the center of the circle. Participants standing on the spots are each given a number. The "it" can call out any number or multiple numbers. At that point, participants with that number(s) have to find a new spot on which to stand. The "it" can also yell, "Water spot," which is a signal for everyone to find a new spot. Among all of this confusion, as people are finding a new place to stand, the "it" tries to find a spot for himself, which will cause someone else to be "it" for the next round.

Rules: Once a person is on his spot, he cannot be forced off of it. If two people are going toward a spot at the same time, the first person to get closest (within 12 inches) to the spot takes ownership of it. At that point, the other person has to find a new spot.

Preparation: The activity requires vinyl spots to place on the bottom of the pool.

Number of Participants: A group up to 20 people

Age Range and Swimming Level of Participants: Ages eight and older who have strong swimming skills

Safety Precautions: Participants should use caution and slow down as they approach a spot, in order to avoid slipping on the pool floor.

Game #88: Sea Monster

Objective: To engage in a game that emphasizes deduction and reason through the process of elimination

Goals of Participants: To avoid getting eliminated from the game by the sea monster

Overview: The participants hold hands in a circle in the shallow-end of the swimming pool. Before the game begins, one person is told by an adult leader that the individual will serve as the activity's first "sea monster." This individual tries to secretly eliminate other participants by squeezing the hand of the person located on either side of him, who then passes the hand-squeeze on to the sea monster's intended victim. For example, if the "sea monster" wants to eliminate the seventh person on his left, he would squeeze the individual's hand on his left seven times. That person would then continue the process by squeezing the hand of his neighbor on his left side six times. Subsequently, the next person in line would get five squeezes and so on until the seventh person receives one hand-squeeze at which point, that individual would then be out of the game. The hands of all of the participants are held underwater during the activity in order to make it difficult to trace back the hand-squeezes to the "sea monster."

Rules: A participant, at any time, can make an accusation of whom he thinks the "sea monster" is. If he accuses the wrong person, he is out of the game. The "sea monster" has to answer honestly when he is asked by another participant if he is the "sea monster."

Preparation: A "sea monster" should be selected without anyone else knowing this person's secret identity.

Number of Participants: A group up to 25 people

Age Range and Swimming Level of Participants: Ages eight and older; non-swimmers can participate in the activity.

Safety Precautions: All participants should be cautioned not to squeeze the hand of the people next them too hard.

Game #89: Sea Captain

Objective: To develop listening skills and the ability to be responsive in a quick and efficient manner

Goals of Participants: To follow orders and avoid being eliminated from the game

Overview: Participants are positioned in the shallow-end of the swimming pool. One participant, who is designated the "sea captain," determines what the other participants do by giving five commands in random order. If a participant fails to follow the captain's orders in a timely fashion, that person is eliminated from the game. The game is played until an overall winner is determined.

The five commands that the "sea captain" will issue are:

- "Man your stations!" Everyone must go to the same station, either the bow (front), stern (back), starboard (right), or port (left) of the ship. The captain must specify which station to go to. With this command, the captain is directing all of the participants to go to the same location of the ship. If anyone goes to the wrong station, he is out of the game.
- "Man overboard!" With this command, each participant finds a partner. Both individuals then join hands and hold them in the air. If anyone cannot find a partner quickly, he is out of the game.
- "Go to the Galley (the kitchen on the ship)!" With this command, each participant finds a group of eight people, and together they pretend to eat food at the captain's table. Anyone who fails to find a group of eight is out of the game. It should be noted that this command can only be used at the beginning of the game, when the group is larger than eight people.
- "Attention" and "At ease!" With this command, all participants stand in a line in a straight and upright position. When the captain states, "At ease," all participants should remain in a line formation, but assume a relaxed position. The captain can dismiss anyone who doesn't snap to attention or falls out of the line formation.
- "Hit the deck!" With this command, all participants put their head underwater for one second and then come right back up. Anyone who hesitates in carrying out this command or is underwater longer than five seconds is eliminated from the game.

Rules: Each command eliminates a few participants from the game. Those participants who are no longer playing should wait on the pool deck for a new round of the game to start, in order to make it easier for the captain to know who is currently playing the game.

Preparation: A new captain needs to be picked at the beginning of each round of the game. Where the front of the ship is in the pool should also be determined.

Number of Participants: Up to 30 people

Age Range and Swimming Level of Participants: Ages eight and older, who have strong swimming skills

Safety Precautions: Participants should be cautioned to watch out for other participants who might be doing the same maneuver in order to prevent colliding with them.

Game #90: Musical Islands

Objective: To teach assertiveness during the game, while continuing to exhibit good sportsmanship and kindness

Goals of Participants: To visit all of the "islands" while the music is playing and to find an island once the music stops and stay there until the music resumes

Overview: Vinyl spots are placed on the floor of the shallow-end of the pool in a large circle, with one less vinyl spot than the number of participants. These spots represent "islands" that participants walk on when Hawaiian music is playing. When the music stops, everyone scrambles to find an "island" on which to stand.

Rules: Only one person can stand on an island. The participant who doesn't have an island to stand on is out of the game. When a person leaves the game, one of the "islands" is removed to always have one less "island" than people. If two participants are going toward the same "island" at the same time, the first individual to get closest (within 12 inches) to the "island" takes ownership of it. As such, the other person has to find a new "island." The game is played until an overall winner is determined.

Preparation: A CD of Hawaiian music is played and randomly stopped during the activity.

Number of Participants: Up to 20 people

Age Range and Swimming Level of Participants: Ages eight and older who have strong swimming skills

Safety Precautions: Participants should use caution and slow down as they approach a vinyl spot in order to avoid slipping on the pool floor.

9

Floating Board Games and Puzzles

Game #91: Foam Dominoes

Objective: To build teamwork

Goals of Participants: To set up foam dominoes on the water as quickly as possible

Overview: In the shallow-end of the swimming pool, the group is divided into smaller teams. Each team is given foam dominoes that float on the water. Team members then race against the clock to lay out the dominoes on the water's surface. The number of dots at the end of each domino needs to match up with the same number on an adjacent domino. If the end of the domino is blank, that domino also needs to be matched up to another blank domino. The team that can accomplish this task the fastest wins the game.

Rules: One particular challenge that the team will face is that the dominoes float away if they're not held in place by team members.

Preparation: The activity requires a set of large foam dominoes and a stopwatch.

Number of Participants: A team of up to 20 people

Age Range and Swimming Level of Participants: Ages eight and older; non-swimmers can participate in the activity.

Safety Precautions: An adult leader should be positioned in the pool to retrieve any dominoes that drift into the deep-end of the pool.

Game #92: Foam Tic-Tac-Toe

Objective: To teach leadership

Goals of Participants: To compete in a game of tic-tac-toe in a water setting

Overview: Using nine-inch foam Xs and Os, two six-member teams play a game of tic-tac-toe in the shallow-end of the swimming pool. One person on the team serves as the captain, and each of the other five team members have an X or O that they place in the playing area. When it is a team's turn, the team captain tells his teammates where their placement should be. Each team member then walks to that location with their foam X or O and stands near it so it doesn't float away.

Rules: The teams flip a coin to see which goes first. The team that initiates the game puts their X or O in the center of the playing area to establish the boundaries of the game. The other players can then put an X or O around the center section. Both teams alternate back and forth, attempting to block the advancement of their opponents, while at the same time trying to put their own letters in a row (i.e., vertical, horizontal, and diagonal rows). The first team to have three letters in a row wins the game. If the game ends in a tie, both teams play again.

Preparation: The activity requires a set of nine-inch foam Xs and Os (five of each).

Number of Participants: Two teams of six players

Age Range and Swimming Level of Participants: Ages six and older; non-swimmers can participate in the activity.

Safety Precautions: An adult leader should be positioned in the pool to retrieve any foam letters that drift into the deep-end of the pool.

Game #93: Foam Puzzle

Objective: To involve a whole team of participants in an effort to accomplish a two-part task

Goals of Participants: To retrieve floating puzzle pieces to put a puzzle together as fast as possible

Overview: Pieces of a foam puzzle are scattered throughout the shallow-end of the swimming pool. A team of five participants then scramble around the pool searching and retrieving puzzle pieces in an attempt to put them together on the water's surface.

Rules: Using a stopwatch, an adult leader times the efforts of each team. The team with the fastest time wins the game.

Preparation: The activity requires a foam puzzle and a stopwatch.

Number of Participants: Teams of up to five people

Age Range and Swimming Level of Participants: Ages eight and older who have strong swimming skills

Safety Precautions: An adult leader should be positioned in the pool to retrieve any puzzle pieces that drift into the deep-end of the pool.

Game #94: Mini Lifeguard Tower

Objective: To exhibit creativity when completing an assigned task as fast as possible

Goals of Participants: To build a miniature lifeguard tower, while standing in the swimming pool

Overview: The group is divided into teams in the shallow-end of the pool. Each team takes a turn and is given five minutes to find floating building materials to build a miniature lifeguard tower out of Tinkertoys®.

Rules: Three adult leaders, serving as judges for this event, award a bag of Swedish Fish candy to the winning team, based on the design and style of the team's construction efforts.

Preparation: The activity requires a candy prize, a stopwatch, and a can of Tinkertoys for each team.

Number of Participants: Teams of up to six people per team

Age Range and Swimming Level of Participants: Ages eight and older; non-swimmers can participate in the activity.

Safety Precautions: The teams perform this task one at a time. All building materials should be counted in advance, so that all pieces are accounted for at the end of the game. The objective is to keep toy parts from collecting in the skimmer baskets or clog the filtration system. An adult leader should be positioned in the pool to retrieve any toy parts that drift into the deep-end of the pool.

Game #95: Floating Velcro Darts

Objective: To utilize imagination when playing a modified game of darts

Goals of Participants: To toss Velcro darts onto a floating Velcro dartboard

Overview: Participants stand six feet from a Velcro dartboard in the shallow-end of the swimming pool. They toss the Velcro balls (darts) onto the dartboard, trying to achieve the highest score by hitting closest to the bull's-eye on the dartboard.

Rules: The floating dartboard lays flat on the water. The participant with the highest score after tossing all of his darts wins that round of the game.

Preparation: The activity requires a Velcro dartboard and a set of Velcro darts. If the dartboard doesn't float on its own, it should be placed on a kickboard.

Number of Participants: Up to six players

Age Range and Swimming Level of Participants: Ages eight and older; non-swimmers can participate in the activity.

Safety Precautions: An adult leader should be positioned in the pool to retrieve any Velcro darts that drift into the deep-end of the pool.

Game #96: Underwater Checkers

Objective: To incorporate an underwater swimming maneuver in the game of checkers

Goals of Participants: To play checkers in the swimming pool

Overview: Two participants play checkers on a floating checkerboard that is positioned in the shallow-end of the swimming pool. The checkerboard lies on top of a kickboard that is floating on the water. Participants cannot hold the checkerboard in place, but have to continue moving around the pool wherever the checkerboard drifts in the shallow-section.

Rules: Anytime a player jumps his opponent's checker to advance in the game, this move only counts if he can also swim under the checkerboard without moving any of the checkers on the board. If the player attempting to swim under the checkerboard completely tips over the checkerboard, the other person automatically wins the game. The first person to jump all of his opponent's checkers and swim under the checkerboard each time successfully wins the game.

Preparation: The activity requires a game of checkers and a kickboard.

Number of Participants: Two players

Age Range and Swimming Level of Participants: Ages eight and older who have strong swimming skills

Safety Precautions: An adult leader should be positioned in the pool to retrieve the checkerboard, the kickboard, and any checkers that drift into the deep-end of the pool.

Game #97: Floating Dice Game

Objective: To try to anticipate what the roll of the dice will bring

Goals of Participants: To be at the right "spot" at the right time

Overview: Six vinyl spots are placed on the floor in a circle in the shallow-end of the pool. Each vinyl spot has a number on it, ranging from one to six. Music plays, while all participants walk in the circle. When the music stops, everyone stands near a numbered spot. Then, an adult leader throws a large foam die onto the water. Whatever the number is on the die, the individual standing on that numbered spot is out of the game. The music then resumes, and participants continue the same routine. Another possibility would be to utilize a pair of dice to eliminate two groups of people at the same time by using both numbers.

Rules: A fun way to end the game would be to have an adult leader roll the die and whatever the number on the die comes up is the winning number. The group standing near that numbered spot wins the game, and all other numbers and groups are eliminated from the game.

Preparation: The activity requires six numbered vinyl spots and a pair of large foam dice.

Number of Participants: Up to 25 people

Age Range and Swimming Level of Participants: Ages eight and older, non-swimmers can participate in the activity.

Safety Precautions: Participants should use caution and slow down as they approach a vinyl spot in order to avoid slipping on the pool floor.

10

Rainy Days

#98: Baby Shark Song

Objective: To sing a song while participants are waiting for the pool to open

Goals of Participants: To keep warm on a rainy day by singing a song and simultaneously performing hand actions

Overview:

Lyrics	Hand Actions
Baby shark Doot Doot . . . Doot . . . Doot	(thumb and index finger open and close)
Toddler shark Doot Doot . . . Doot . . . Doot	(thumb and all of the fingers open and close)
Child shark Doot Doot . . . Doot . . . Doot	(two hands clap together)
Teen shark Doot Doot . . . Doot . . . Doot	(two arms put together at the elbows to open and close)
Mama shark Doot Doot . . . Doot . . . Doot	(both arms open and close wide)
Daddy shark Doot Doot . . . Doot . . . Doot	(both arms open and close even wider)
Monster shark Doot Doot . . . Doot . . . Doot	(one arm and one leg moving up and down together)
Grandpa shark Doot Doot . . . Doot . . . Doot	(two hands clap together, with the fingers folded in to represent no teeth)
Man swimming Doot Doot . . . Doot . . . Doot	(both arms make swimming motion)
Shark attack Doot Doot . . . Doot . . . Doot	(one hand over the head to look like a shark fin)
Man swims faster Doot Doot . . . Doot . . . Doot	(faster swimming motion)
Man gets away Doot Doot . . . Doot Doot . . . Doot Doot . . . Doot . . . Doot	(snap fingers four times)

Rules: An adult leader sings the song the first time, and all participants sing it the second time.

Preparation: If it is raining, the activity should be conducted in a dry place, like a pavilion.

Number of Participants: A group of two and more people; the game is ideal for large groups.

Age Range and Swimming Level of Participants: Ages six and older; non-swimmers can participate in the activity.

Safety Precautions: Participants should be spaced out far enough so that no one gets hit with flinging arms and legs.

Game #99: Waterfall

Objective: To develop teamwork and cooperation

Goals of Participants: To collectively pick up a bucket of water and dump it into another bucket

Overview: Team members each hold onto a string that is connected to a bungee cord. As each participant pulls back on his string, the bungee cord expands. The team collectively places the cord over the top of a one-gallon bucket to transport it and dump the water in it into a three-gallon bucket.

Rules: If the team spills any water, they have to start the process over again.

Preparation: The activity requires eight six-foot pieces of rope tied to a bungee cord that is in a loop, a one-gallon bucket (filled with water), and an empty three-gallon bucket.

Number of Participants: Up to eight people

Age Range and Swimming Level of Participants: Ages six and older; non-swimmers can participate in the activity.

Safety Precautions: If this activity is held on the swimming pool deck, it should be conducted far enough away from walkways around the pool to avoid becoming a tripping hazard.

Game #100: Go Fish

Objective: To provide the opportunity to play an aquatic-themed game in the area adjacent to the pool

Goals of Participants: To collect cards of the same value

Overview: Each participant gets seven playing cards and then attempts to collect four of these cards with the same value. When four cards of the same value are collected by an individual, he lays them down, face up, and then continues collecting sets of four until he runs out of cards.

Rules: In an attempt to get a set of four cards, a player, when it is his turn, asks another player if he has the desired card. If his colleague does not have that card, the requesting player has to "Go fish," which requires him to draw from a pile of cards positioned in the center of the playing area. The game continues until either one player runs out of cards or the pile of cards in the center is depleted. The player who is out of cards wins the game. If the pile in the center runs out, then a new round of the game is started after the deck of cards has been completely shuffled and distributed to each player.

Preparation: The activity requires a deck of 52 playing cards.

Number of Participants: Two to five players

Age Range and Swimming Level of Participants: Ages six and older; non-swimmers can participate in the activity.

Safety Precautions: If this game is played in the pool area, participants should not interfere with the lifeguard's duties and responsibilities.

Game #101: Cup Game

Objective: To provide an opportunity to play a rainy-day game that is designed to teach patience and enhance motor skills and memory

Goals of Participants: To stay in the game by being exact in all of the required cup movements

Overview: Participants sit at a table, each behind a plastic cup. Simultaneously, in a rhythmic motion, each participant places his cup upside down. He then claps twice and taps on the top of the cup three times. At which point, the cup is moved to the individual on the participant's right, who then claps once and puts the cup he just received from the person on his left in an upright position. Next, he taps the cup with his right hand and sets it back in an upside-down position. Finally, he grabs the cup with his right hand, while crossing over his left hand, places it in an upright position, and claps three times.

Rules: When a participant does a wrong maneuver or does not stay in step with the rest of the group, he is eliminated from the game. The game is played until an overall winner is determined.

Preparation: The activity requires a durable plastic cup for each participant.

Number of Participants: Three or more people; the game is ideal for a large group

Age Range and Swimming Level of Participants: Ages eight and older; non-swimmers can participate in the activity.

Safety Precautions: Participants should be cautioned to not slam the cups down on the table in order to prevent possible injuries.

About the Author

Since 1996, Jared R. Knight has been a member of the staff at Aspen Grove Family Camp, owned by Brigham Young University, where he currently serves as the manager of programs and human resources. In this position, he supervises programs and activities for more than 5,000 children during summer camp and autumn weekend events. He also develops winter programming for 3,500 teenagers, providing faith-based youth conferences, in which he organizes cross-country skiing and snowshoeing outings.

In preparing for this book, Knight used his experiences as a former Walt Disney World cast member, college intramural sports supervisor/referee, certified pool operator, American Red Cross health and safety instructor, and lifeguard to develop many of the ideas for the games included in this text.

Knight is the president of the Southwest Section of the American Camp Association. He is the author of several well-received books, including 101 Creative Programs for Children, 101 Age-Appropriate Camp Activities, and 101 Games and Activities to Strengthen Families. He is also the featured presenter of a 13-part DVD series on recreational programming.

Knight received a bachelor's degree in recreation management and youth leadership and a master's degree in public administration from Brigham Young University. He has also served as the director of development for United Way of Utah County and as a camp director for the Boy Scouts of America.

Knight and his wife, LaDonna, live in Utah with their three children, Rachel, Alex, and Emerson.